301.18
AVi

9077

HM
133
A88

Avis, Warren E
Shared participations

DATE DUE

FEB 28 1986

Shared Participation

Shared Participation

Finding Group Solutions to Personal, Corporate and Community Problems

BY WARREN E. AVIS

DOUBLEDAY & COMPANY, INC.
GARDEN CITY, NEW YORK
1973

COLLEGE FOR HUMAN SERVICES
LIBRARY
345 HUDSON STREET
NEW YORK, N.Y. 10014

ISBN: 0-385-05904-3
Library of Congress Catalog Card Number 72-76117
Copyright © 1973 by Warren E. Avis
All Rights Reserved
Printed in the United States of America
First Edition

Acknowledgments

This book could not have been written without the many who contributed their time and creative talent to help us in our goal of developing systems and programs to achieve better understanding between individuals, groups, communities, and society in general.

From business, from industry, from the academic world, from government, and the man in the street, we have received understanding, help, encouragement, acceptance and the input of creative ideas. These people have made our efforts satisfying and rewarding.

Acknowledgments

From the ranks of government, we have been encouraged by the participation of many people—policemen on the beat to ambassadors. My thanks go out to Guilford Dudley, former U.S. ambassador to Denmark, now Chairman of the Board of Life and Casualty Co., who sent executive sales force personnel through one or more of our programs, and to his Executive Vice-President, Bob Zelle (now president of the G. T. Corporation), who helped develop many of the problem-solving techniques now incorporated in our program.

The Detroit Police Department has been a loyal and consistent supporter since the beginning. We have enjoyed the input and feedback received from Inspector Robert Quaid, Director of Training; Superintendent of Police Charles H. Gentry, who is now Chief of Police of Port Huron, Michigan; Inspector Delore L. Ricard, Executive Assistant to the Commissioner; Inspector Theodore S. Siensky, Director of the Administrative Services Bureau; Inspector Dorothy Gay, Inspector of the Women's Division, and William Hanger, Chief of Police of Pontiac, Michigan—all of whom have evidenced their great interest in new methods to improve community relations and person-to-person communication.

From the Academic Community, we have received valuable assistance. Dr. C. D. DeLisle Crawford, Professor of Education at Wayne State University, who evaluated our programs, worked with us and gave college credits to people who participated in the Lab. Dr. C. H. Lindquist, President of Bethel College and Seminary, St. Paul, Minnesota, sent us several of his top aides and helped us in formulating our program. Lord Mountbatten, President of

Acknowledgments vii

the Council for United World College, sent us his key personnel. Their feedback was beneficial and is appreciated. Dr. Roland DeMarco, former President of Finch College and now head of the Korean Relief Fund, attended and then contributed his time and enthusiasm to our program, and, on occasion, generously made the facilities of Finch College available to us.

From the business community, Lida Livingston, President of Livingston Communications, Inc., participated in one of our programs, sent us several of her associates, and, more, has contributed by editing our material, lecturing on our program, and promoting expansion of our activities. Also from the business community, I want to give a special word of appreciation to Elmer Johns, former Personnel Director of General Mills, who now has his own company, Elmer Johns Associates, and who has participated in our program, sent his aides to participate in the lab experience, and helped us to evolve our "Personality Coin."

Fred Wacker, President of Ammco Tools Inc., a personal friend who attended one of our first programs, has been extremely helpful since the beginning. The Honorable Walter G. Arader, Secretary of the Department of Commerce, State of Pennsylvania, has given us continuing support since attending a program and has sent us several of the key people of his department.

A special note of appreciation is due Molly Black, of our staff, who has been enthusiastic throughout; has helped us put our program together, and has been a strong influence in making our programs successful. Space does not allow me to express thanks to all those to whom I owe thanks, but I must include a special thanks to Maggie Wells and

Richard Curtis, for their invaluable assistance in the writing of this book, and also to Julie Coopersmith, Doubleday editor, who first *saw* a book in Shared Participation, and who argued and encouraged me into starting and finishing it. To all the unnamed ones, you know you have my personal appreciation. If, with the help of these people, we have helped lessen man's inhumanity to man by even one iota, we have been rewarded—and we are sure they are also.

Contents

	Introduction	1
I	Strangers in a Circle	9
II	Let Your Ego Take Five	28
III	How to Succeed in Business Without Really Lying	45
IV	Shared Participation	61
V	Charting a Course Through Life	80
VI	We Can All Be Heroes	98
VII	A Company Is Not a Building	115
VIII	Taking Personal Inventory	130
IX	You've Got to Start at the Top	144
X	Love Thy Neighbor—and Thyself	158
	Appendix	171

Shared Participation

Introduction

After selling the company I had founded in 1946, Avis Rent-A-Car, I discovered that there are some problems that money, even millions, cannot cure. It is a sad truth that often only the affluent have the luxury of exploring personal problems.

But it seems that in those frenzied years I had lost touch with my inner self. I didn't know who I was, who I wanted to be, where I was going. "Tut, tut," I hear cynics clucking, "poor Avis cried all the way to the bank." It might be possible to be content with the power and material comfort that money brings, and seek no further. But in my own system of values, this is not enough. I wanted to make a contribution to society, to do something altruistic, to make a commitment to a cause higher than a rum collins by the side of a posh resort pool. In fact, I believe it is particularly incumbent on those fortunate enough to have made a lot of money, for they have the resources, the influence, and the leverage to do good that persons of more modest means simply cannot hope to have. We have the luxury and the time to try to understand what is happening in society. And we have an obligation to try to find a way by which the various groups in this world can communicate. Communication is after all, the key to understanding.

For me, an identity crisis coupled with substantial means led me onto pathways that finally emerged on the broad avenue of personal fulfillment. Its name was behavioral science. Through it I not only learned who Warren Avis was, but what he could do with his life that would enable him to feel it had been purposeful and meaningful.

I am an original member of the Young President's Organization, a group of executives dedicated to developing and applying good ideas and values in the business community. One day I was invited to participate in an experiment with some other Young Presidents, a sensitivity training laboratory. Sensitivity training at that time was still in the embryonic stage, but the purpose of the session was certainly something YPO members could sympathize with: how to make business executives both more effective as persons and more sensitive to the needs of their families, friends, business associates and customers.

Crude and brief though that first "encounter" was, I came away from it flabbergasted at how much I had learned about myself. The biggest shock of all was the realization of how little I had heard, all those years, of the emotional needs of those around me. Why had I never really listened to the needs of others and how on earth, I wondered, had I managed to achieve even a fraction of success with the blinders I'd been wearing? To this day I'm still at a loss to explain it.

A great many people who discover themselves that way in a laboratory emerge with a crusading spirit and want everyone they know to drop what they are doing and hie themselves to a group. I was not so fanatical, but I did recognize two things: that the experience could be invaluable to anyone who gave it a chance, and that I had the time, money, energy and determination to make the facilities and techniques of behavioral science available to a wider range of people. I saw two important results of a behavioral science center. First, by bringing in leaders of the business, social, political, educational, religious, and other fields, and teaching them how to face themselves as well as those around them, we could effect significant changes in the structures and attitudes of their institutions. And by bringing in those who did not play leadership roles and who often had similar difficulties in relating, but who hadn't always learned effective techniques of using their human potential, we could achieve a broader base of understanding among a great variety of individuals, and perhaps filter that understanding down through every level of society.

It almost sounds as if I was creating a revolutionary party. And indeed you might say that I was, only the revolution was not political. It was emotional and even spiritual. It was a revolution of people's viewpoints.

I thus created the American Behavioral Science Training Laboratories, funding the center in Ann Arbor, Michigan. The key word in our title was to be *science*. My investigations had revealed that sensitivity training up to that time was pretty much geared to increasing awareness only on an interpersonal basis, was frequently conducted by persons of little professional psychological background, and often experimented with human emotions without controls and without any idea of what the results might be. There were no statistics on effectiveness of techniques, and no follow-up on long-term results. In short, there was no science, and from my observations, those are still the prevailing approaches in most "encounter," "sensitivity," and similar groups.

The lab I founded, ABS—rhymes with "labs"—thus departed from the so-called "Feel Me, Touch Me, Hold Me" approach in its efforts to classify all techniques and codify all results in a scientific fashion. Toward that end we brought in top behavioral scientists and now employ up-to-date computerized programs and evaluations in assessing the progress of group members.

Our Detroit laboratories are held in a spacious, comfortable suburban motel. If you join one of our groups you'll be coupled with a roommate of your own sex who is also a lab participant. This stranger will have been selected deliberately for you, and vice versa, on the basis of compatibility of character. By "compatibility" I don't necessarily mean that the two of you have identical interests. Far to the contrary, on the surface of it you may seem to be as far apart temperamentally as two people can be. We've had a police official with a homosexual, a hippie radical with a conservative business executive, a housewife with a social butterfly. Yet as the labs progress and you start communicating with your roommate, you realize how much he or she has to offer you, and how much you are offering in return. By the same token you discover how much you have deprived yourself of in your life by closing yourself to people who are—superficially—different from yourself.

Approximately ten of you will meet with a "trainer," as the leader is known, for six days and evenings. You will not know each other, and last names and occupations will not be revealed to you until the end of the sessions. Though it will be obvious to you at the outset that the group is made up of people of different ages, occupations, and ways of life, you will have no way of knowing those factors until the last day or two. Marks of status, wealth, and social position are nowhere in evidence, for you'll all have been asked to wear simple clothing and to shed anything—love beads, a lodge pin, an expensive ring—which might give the other members clues to your identity.

But how, you probably ask with some anxiety, is anyone going to know who you are if you're bereft of those comfortable symbols? Well, as soon as you ask that question your involvement in the lab has begun, for it's in that area of symbols—"first impressions"—that so many relationships get off on the wrong foot.

To prove it, one of the first things you'll be asked to do in your first session is write down your assumptions about the other members of the group. "Oh, she's a socialite for sure," you'll say to yourself, "and he's a traveling salesman if I ever saw one, and that one's a hippie and the other is a football player." When your assumptions are read back to you toward the end of the sessions, you'll be astonished how far off base many of them were and how your perceptions have changed. The socialite may turn out to be a welfare administrator, the traveling salesman a schoolteacher, the hippie a business executive, and the ballplayer—a socialite!

In the pleasant surroundings of the group's conference suite in the motel, you'll be given a number of other written "tests" to chart your progress, and there will also be some non-verbal exercises aimed at revealing trust or distrust, warmth or indifference, anxiety or comfort, etc. Naturally, you will feel some uneasiness, for you've been removed from a familiar environment to one bristling with unknowns. Will I say the wrong thing? Will they think I'm a fool or a heel or a mouse? How am I ever going to show them who the real me is? What will happen to me if I lose my temper?

Your nervousness is, I admit, somewhat justified, for you and your labmates will be encouraged to speak about each other forthrightly, and sometimes the candor can be brutal. "Why do you always speak in such a monotonous voice?" someone may ask you. Or, "Can't you say one sentence without referring to 'your staff'?"

Introduction

Or, "How come you're always knocking the government? Did it ever occur to you it's not the country that's all messed up, it's *you?*"

You may even be miserable at first, but after the first wave of resentment passes, you'll realize that something wonderful has happened: you've faced a truth about yourself that you've never been required to face before. You'll have identified, with the help of the other lab members, a problem in yourself, perceived its cause, and even helped yourself develop a solution. Even more wonderful, you'll find that you've done the same for your colleagues in the lab!

The broader application of this process can be seen in the problem-solving operation we call "Shared Participation." Members of a group contribute information and suggest solutions to a specific problem. These aren't labeled as to their source, and solutions from persons untrained in a field are thus discussed as fully as those put forth by experts. The solution reached is a voluntary consensus of the group and most often not one of the original suggestions at all, but a new one or an amalgam that evolved out of the ensuing discussions. The degree of commitment of all the members of a group to the solution arrived at by this means is, ABS has discovered, exceptionally high.

Shared Participation is a technique that can be invaluable in solving problems within a firm or organization, university, community, anywhere. Indeed, I do not believe it unrealistic to imagine that the experience can help solve society's problems, right up to the most challenging one of all, war.

Introduction

But even on the most fundamental level, namely that of individual effectiveness, the lab experience is of inestimable value. For all of us go through life like a boat through uncharted waters, with only the most primitive instruments to tell us where the waters are shoal, where the dangerous obstructions are, what sort of squalls and seas we might expect. As a society we have to put charts into the hands of participants, and outfit them with at least sufficient instrumentation—in the form of self-understanding, sensitivity, and increased effectiveness—to avoid the bad water and weather as far as that is possible in life. As people we must learn to listen to others and learn to overcome misunderstanding, egoism, and self-interest. The Shared Participation method, whether it be used in the family, the business, the community, or the larger arena of world politics offers some hope to avoid the conflicts and disturbances which have become the hallmarks of our time.

I. Strangers in a Circle

What do a man and a can of soup have in common? A label. The soup label tells the story of the brand and the kind of soup. A man's label can be as blatant as a badge or a string of love beads; as subtle as a famous surname or an old school tie.

For the most part, we wear our labels proudly. They represent the public identities we've selected for ourselves and worked to establish over the years, and we use them as calling cards for society's approval. At the same time, we also hide behind these labels, and by doing

Shared Participation

so, we deprive ourselves of many vital sources of self-knowledge.

Self-knowledge has been one of man's primary goals for a long, long time. The ancient Greeks preached, "Know thyself." Countless legends have been woven around the idea of royal personages disguising themselves as commoners and roaming the streets, talking with strangers, to find out what their subjects truly think of them. These legends are the roots of behavioral science, for they are based on an inescapable fact of life: If a man wearing a crown stops a peasant and asks him if he thinks he's doing a good job, the answer is predictable. It works the same way with any easily identifiable label. For example, a priest wearing a clerical collar cannot expect candid or unrestrained criticism from a member of the faith he serves.

Anonymity is thus the key to the behavioral science process known as Shared Participation. In Shared Participation a lab group will attack a given problem by submitting solutions anonymously. The solutions are read, considered, debated, and voted on. Everyone in the group *participates* in coming to an answer; everyone *shares* the benefits of the lab group's collective efforts. The solution is therefore larger than the sum of its parts. It may be a modification of one of the proposed solutions, or an amalgam of all of them, or a totally new idea inspired by the group dialogue. But it is always one in which all of the members are involved, one they are proud of, one they are committed to.

Shared Participation owes its success to the fact that nobody in the group knows who suggested what. The reasoning is that a genuinely good idea is often lost when members of an organization are playing power politics, taking ego trips, performing roles, or seeking status. But it will never be lost when all of this game-playing equipment is hurled into a sea of anonymity. If you know you can get fired for criticizing your boss's idea, you'll think twice. But if you don't know it's his, you will give your criticism freely. And if *you* are a boss, you will be much more inclined to accept suggestions whose origins you're not sure of, because your status weapons will have been taken away from you.

We've all had the experience of getting into conversation with a stranger while traveling, or even sitting in the park. We find ourselves suddenly baring secrets and letting our hair down in a way we wouldn't dream of doing with an acquaintance or even a close friend. One of the times it happened to me was during a plane trip from Detroit to Los Angeles. To pass the time, I struck up a conversation with my seatmate, a well-dressed man in his forties whom I'll call Jim Henderson. It wasn't until we landed that he gave me his business card, and I learned that he was the sales manager of a company in Cleveland with which I had had some contacts.

During our flight, Henderson related a fascinating but tragic story concerning the illness of his fourteen-year-old daughter. The child was afflicted with an incurable but controllable kidney disease, and the cost of the dialysis treatments that sustained her life were draining the family's financial resources to the point of desperation. Henderson was worrying himself sick, thinking ahead to the time when his savings would be depleted and he would have to look for another way to finance the lifesaving treatments. The strain was increased by his efforts to keep his worries to himself and avoid letting them show to his wife or their daughter.

Some weeks later, I happened to meet the president of the corporation for which Henderson worked. During the course of a luncheon conversation, I related Henderson's story to him. It was as I'd suspected; he was obviously astonished to hear it. Henderson had never confided his troubles to anyone at the plant. But as the company president thought it over, he remarked that the story helped to explain a noticeable change in Henderson's work—a change which was just barely beginning to show up on the firm's sales charts. Frankly, I don't know how Henderson's story ended, but I like to think that having the truth about his difficulties come out—through a chance encounter with a stranger on an airplane—helped to alleviate his problem.

The freedom with which we bare our souls to strangers proves something that behavioral scientists have known for years—that anonymity is the key to self-knowledge. Anonymity is the keystone of behavioral science, which is the best tool man has yet devised for the purpose of getting to know himself better. Behavioral science gives us the gift the poet Robert Burns yearned for in verse— "to see oursel's as others see us." But to see ourselves clearly, we must come out of hiding behind our labels and face each other as strangers.

Behavioral science is based on the assumption that everybody wishes to improve himself, to grow, to become a better person. Of course, some people pursue this goal much more sensibly than others do. There are many people in whom the desire for self-improvement is scarcely discernible, and others in whom it seems to have petered out completely. But at some point in our lives, we all wish to better our lots. As we grow older, the urge to improve oneself may diminish into a simple desire to preserve the status quo by not becoming a worse person. This can also require a great effort. And how can one achieve any degree of self-improvement without having a true image of oneself from which to start?

We can kid ourselves that we get a pretty clear picture of what we're like from our friends and family, but this is not a very realistic way of looking at things. "Even your best friends won't tell you!" Remember that old slogan? Well, it applies to a lot of things besides dandruff or bad breath. It's a common course of behavior for one's family, friends and fellow workers to try to accept us as we are, taking the bad with the good. If they see faults, they try to ignore them. Out of love or lesser emotions, such as fear or envy, they feel they may have too much to lose by being honest. In other situations, we block out criticism from those who are closest to us. We can't bear the thought that our faults—large or small—are visible to these people we care so much about, so we deny the existence of those faults. And in still other cases, when one member of a family habitually nags another, these complaints go unheeded for another reason. With constant repetition, the complaints lose their impact and take on the monotony of a chant.

This is where the behavioral science laboratory has

the advantage, for it provides an environment of absolute anonymity in which each individual can feel free to discover his true nature without the fetters of familiar relationships or presupposed expectations. The behavioral science laboratory sets up an arena of anonymity where ten strangers come face to face. Nobody is anybody's best friend. Nobody even knows anybody else in the group. So personal evaluation depends entirely upon the reality of a person's being. Status symbols are buried, and previous associations, including one's professional identity, don't count. They are not even revealed. At first, only first names are used, and participants are instructed to wear a common "uniform" of casual clothes. This set of conditions insures maximum anonymity—the only medium in which honest feedback can flourish.

If anonymity is the key to self-discovery, feedback is what pushes the door open. It is the life's blood of the behavioral science lab. Many factors prohibit our receiving honest feedback in our everyday lives. Power, for example, can be a tremendous obstacle to self-discovery. How can anybody in a position of power ever be certain if people like him for himself or if they like him (or pretend to) because of his power? Are they afraid of his power, and does this fear force them to feign admiration? In the behavioral science lab, a powerful person is reduced, at least outwardly, to equality with everybody else, and he can find the true answers to these questions if he really wants to. He is released from the prison of his power because nobody in the group is aware of his position.

A magic circle—that's what the laboratory experience

is, essentially. The magic is provided by the fact that the people, who usually arrange themselves in a rough circle, are total strangers to each other. In the beginning stages, these ten strangers sit still, silently appraising each other and just as silently sharing mutual doubts and fears. They share a sense of hesitation, a very natural reluctance to go first—to be the one to break the ice. But gradually, the silent circle spawns a new force—a group dynamic that can change the lives and the thinking of every member of the group.

This group dynamic is a universal thing, and its power extends to any culture, at any time in history, with any group of people, because it is basically a human dynamic. As the group dynamic moves into gear in the behavioral science laboratory, you can really find out who you are. You can find out who you are because that's all that's showing.

There you sit in your ordinary, casual, unplaceable clothes—identified to the others only as John or Mary or George. You could be a housewife or a physicist or a banker or a policeman or a student or a salesman or a plumber or a teacher. These are your ordinary, everyday labels. But who and what you really are—the actual person who lives behind these labels—will emerge as the laboratory experience gathers momentum. It will come out in what you say and how you react to what others say— both about you and about themselves. As the lab progresses, those nine strangers will be able to see you clearly and without prejudice, and their honest feedback will give you a clearer picture of yourself than you have ever had before or could obtain from any other source.

16   Shared Participation

At ABS for example, we believe in encouraging a free-form exchange for at least the first few days, because this format allows for the widest possible latitude and the greatest potential for self-discovery. Communication within the group is entirely verbal; and sex, politics, and religion are discouraged as topics of conversation. This is done not so much out of fear of controversy or disagreement, but instead, to conserve the group's time and to channel its analytical energies into areas of common interest which are more likely to produce constructive discussions, meaningful communication, and enlightening conclusions.

We are accustomed to using the phrase "the laboratory experience"—but it is something of an understatement. It could more accurately be termed the laboratory adventure, for it is an adventure in self-understanding. The action is continuous and exciting. Personal perspectives shift like so much sand and occasionally change completely during the course of the week-long program. There are no familiar limits or non-limits of behavior and/or authority to threaten or reassure. The touchstones are all brand new, and one's everyday parameters vanish altogether.

The group's only boundary is the group itself, for a laboratory group is only as good as its participants. That is to say, its success is limited by—and can even be predetermined by—the limits of the combined experience of the participants. For this reason, we have found it advantageous when dealing with problems of leadership to incorporate representatives of three major segments of our society—the governmental, business and intellectual communities—into each of our groups. We have discovered that this three-way mix provides the richest material and the widest possible range of knowledge and experience to be applied to the problems encountered by the group.

In the average laboratory group, which numbers ten participants, the individual's knowledge-and-experience quotient is raised to ten. So, like Galahad, one's strength becomes the strength of ten—at least in regard to the potential for understanding and self-discovery. And this potential is insured and enhanced by the anonymous nature of the group—the ingredient that provides for a completely free flow of knowledge and experience from one person to another within the group.

What can the cop and the hippie-student learn from each other? On the street, or during a campus confrontation, nothing. In those circumstances, each is hampered by preconceived opinions which tend to prejudice rational judgments and produce mutual distrust. In the atmosphere of the behavioral science laboratory, the two people are forced into a neutral zone of anonymity and are compelled to regard each other as human beings. They don't recognize each other as a "cop" and a "hippie" —and unless they watch out, they may even emerge from the experience fast friends.

"Laboratory training" is a common term used in the behavioral science field. We prefer to call our sessions teaching experiences or learning experiences, rather than refer to them as training labs, because they are not truly training programs, yet they provide the participants with many valuable lessons.

In the company of total strangers, one can learn a great deal. One learns that one is not alone, and comes to understand that the experiences we have hitherto considered unique (and for this reason, worrying or threatening) have been shared all along by others. In this way, one can learn to accept hard truths about oneself. Even more important, one can learn to listen to other people. This is a very hard lesson for most of us to learn. To really listen well, we must be able to hear beyond the words that are uttered. We must hear the real messages that lie behind those words. We must learn to be able to tell when "no" means "yes," and when "yes" means "maybe." Here again, anonymity is the key to understanding and clear perception.

Take that important, powerful person we were talking about earlier—say, the president of a large corporation. Surrounded by yes-men, this gentleman may not hear an honest statement from one end of the fiscal year to another. At the same time, basking in his own importance, this same gentleman may fail to hear the hidden, truthful messages that lie behind the words his subordinates actually say to him. Unconsciously, the unheeding tycoon and his spineless subordinates conspire to check the flow of vital information between them; they manage to shield the tycoon from any kind of disturbing knowledge —about himself or the company. In the laboratory, it's different. A conspiracy of truth replaces the conspiracy of comfort or convenience.

In the laboratory, the corporate president's stranger-companions suffer no compunctions in telling a man they know only as George or Ted or John that he's a selfish, self-centered son-of-a-bitch. They have nothing to lose by doing so. And conversely, the executive himself has no status to lose by confiding to the group the loneliness, the overwhelming sense of isolation he feels in his job. Ultimately, the group may help him to see that this is largely a result of his own inability to communicate properly with other officers of his corporation and the workers, too.

You can reverse this dynamic and look at it from the viewpoint of an employee in the lower echelons of a corporation or other organization. Because most such organizations are built on power and status relationships, the guy at the bottom must play a power game in his way just as the one at the top must play one his way. The goal of getting along with the boss sometimes overrides that of doing the job right. Once this attitude begins to pervade a man's thinking, it can cause all kinds of mischief, ranging from trivial mistakes to downright dishonesty. And the strangest thing of all is, this lackeylike behavior doesn't always please the boss. In fact, the employee who devotes most of his energies to pleasing his superior may often find himself canned for lack of initiative. Not every boss is vain enough to want nothing but yes-men around him.

In the lab, the organization underling is intentionally deprived of the touchstones of status. Without such symbols to guide him as limousines, tailor-made suits, corner offices with breathtaking views of the city, and gorgeous secretaries, the lower- or middle-management exec is thrown back on his own resources and must use new criteria for judging how important other people are—

criteria like honesty, integrity, self-respect, and dignity. The result is, when he returns to the job, he's likely to approach it with a whole new set of standards. He may not flatter his boss's ego as much as he used to, but he'll undoubtedly please him in ways that will contribute to the efficiency of the organization.

Another lesson that emerges from the anonymous laboratory setting is a reminder of that old one about not judging a book by its cover. As Sir William Gilbert so aptly put it in *H.M.S. Pinafore*, "Things are seldom what they seem, skim milk masquerades as cream." In a behavioral science laboratory group, the "skim milk" could be a prize-winning bio-chemist who looks like a housewife; a long-haired policeman who looks like a hippie; a gruff-speaking bully who turns out to be afraid of everything and everyone; or a shy, shrinking violet who, in the clinches, displays an iron nerve and a strength of will to match. It takes hours of verbal challenge and interaction to discover who the participants really are—how their strengths and their weaknesses are revealed in their behavior within the group. The results of this discovery can be as surprising as they are illuminating.

Take the case of Mrs. S., a highly sophisticated, very feminine, and extremely successful interior decorator who flew out from her home town, New York City, to participate in a lab session in Ann Arbor. Mrs. S.'s first reaction to her assigned roommate—a brusque, masculine-looking woman whose entire wardrobe seemed to consist of men's clothes—was one of unabashed horror. Yet during the course of the week, Mrs. S. made several discoveries about her roommate—for one thing, "She had never allowed herself to like many people, so she always spoke as though she were giving orders." In other words, her bark was a great deal worse than her bite.

By the final day of the laboratory experience, a communications barrier which at first had appeared to be unbreachable had been breached, and the two women were as friendly as a pair of pally college roommates. One had learned to see through or beyond the surface of another, unlikely-looking human being—to bypass the obvious and discover the worth of the inner person. The other woman had learned to drop her defenses and offer her friendship trustingly to another.

It's a beautiful thing to see mistrust dissolve and understanding take its place. It happened most dramatically at one laboratory session when a police inspector was assigned to share a room with an artist who appeared to be and turned out to be a homosexual. In the beginning the policeman was fearful and suspicious—very uptight about the whole arrangement. But during an early, freeform session, the artist blurted out his whole life story to the group. It was a harrowing tale, and everybody present—including the police inspector—was moved to tears of sympathy and understanding. As the week wore on, the police inspector and the artist managed to surmount their very different personalities and points of view and to become warm friends.

After the laboratory session had come to an end and the police inspector returned to duty at his station house, one of the first things he did was to call his counterpart in the city where the artist lived. To the distant inspector, he explained his encounter with the artist and repeated highlights of the moving narrative he had witnessed; and by the end of the telephone conversation, he had managed to persuade the inspector to contact one of his precinct captains and to order a halt to the police harassment to which the artist had been subjected for many months. And so the laboratory encounter yielded an obvious, positive benefit for the artist—but it was also beneficial for the police inspector. Up until the time he attended the ABS session, this honest, well-meaning cop had been limited by lack of experience. He had simply never sat down and talked to a homosexual in an ordinary, conversational manner. He had never had any real communication with a homosexual. By having this experience at ABS, he was able to gain a new insight and fuller understanding of a human condition to which he had previously paid little attention and, as a result, given little or no consideration.

These are just two examples of the ways in which tolerance levels shift and change when a group of people is cloaked in a collective anonymity. But it is important to remember that this cloak only hides what is unnecessary. It obscures nothing but the label you were wearing before you came in. In the controlled setting of the behavioral science laboratory, everybody becomes Brand X.

In a sense, the laboratory works like a pressure cooker, as the group dynamic forces reality to escape from hiding. One's true traits are driven to the surface by the honesty and the intensity of the verbal interaction. Nobody has anything to lose except some fears, doubts and illusions —the kind of excess baggage we all carry around to some degree. And there is nothing to hamper members of the group from telling you exactly what they think of you. They are in the unique position of being able to tell you precisely how your behavior affects them and to describe the kind of person they judge you to be from observing your behavior. This honest feedback leads you into a new self-awareness which you would not have believed possible before—and which you could not have obtained from any other peer source.

The group forces you to face things about yourself of which you may have been blissfully unaware. Perhaps over the years, you have acquired the habit of using sarcasm as a weapon of defense. You call it having a sense of humor. Under the guise of joking, you have peppered your acquaintances with sarcastic barbs, and they have quite naturally turned away from these verbal volleys, leaving you virtually without any friends.

Now, you can think up dozens of ego-salving reasons to explain to yourself why people don't like you. You can assure yourself that they are jealous of your important position, or envious of your superior intellect, or awed by your accomplishments. But are any of these reasons valid? Much more likely, they are not. But you find it impossible to face the fact that it is nothing more or less than your sarcastic "wit" that has driven away would-be friends.

When a group of strangers levels with you and tells you this, you have to believe it. You are forced to admit that they have no ax to grind, nothing to gain by lying to you or criticizing you unjustly. You see what you didn't see before: Your sarcasm is a drag.

What you do with this new piece of knowledge is up to you. You can continue being sarcastic if you choose—if you like being sarcastic better than you like friends! But at least you have acquired a new insight into your behavior: You know that your sarcasm is the basic cause of your loneliness.

Naturally, the knowledge you acquire in the laboratory is only really valuable if you put it to use in a positive way. Sometimes, the results are more visible than they are at other times, literally. A young girl with a serious weight problem attended an ABS lab during a school vacation. As she approached the dinner table one evening, she asked politely, almost without thinking, if she could sit down. Two people at that particular table quickly replied, "No." One went on to explain to the girl, "You eat like a pig. It makes me sick to my stomach to watch you eat!"

This was shocking news to the girl. Her family had apparently learned to look around her—or maybe they all ate like pigs. At any rate, she took this new piece of knowledge to heart, mended her ways and went on a diet—and subsequently lost forty pounds!

The mirror is the best physical implement man has been able to devise in order to see himself in a true light. A behavioral science laboratory experience is like facing nine absolutely unflattering, uncompromising mirrors. You get undiluted, honest reflections from nine different directions.

Yet most of us, when we think about it, are nine different people or more, rolled into one. One part of us loves to party it up and have a good time, but another part of us loves to curl up at home with a good book; one part of us loves heavy symphonies, but another part loves rock and still another part enjoys those nostalgic "golden oldies"; one part of us enjoys the company of the opposite sex, another likes to mix with one's own. Does that make us schizophrenic? No, just human.

The reason a lab can be so effective is that each of those other nine people in the circle corresponds to one of those people in you, and so each is attuned to one of your wavelengths. When the lab begins to pick up momentum, all of your labmates begin to home in on your various identities.

And you begin to home in on your own identity, the one that encompasses all the others, the one that makes you *you* and nobody else. Shorn of such distractions as status, power, money, identifying clothes, identity gets sorted out from the countless false identities it surrounds itself with.

It's very exciting to discover how you are judged when nobody knows who you are. Of course, the greatest degree of personal discovery is achieved by listening to what the group has to say about you, and accepting their comments as unbiased truth. But valuable insights can also be attained by listening to what you and the group have to say about the other strangers in the circle and weighing how some of these reactions might apply to your own behavior.

The more carefully you listen, the more surprises you may have in store. The careful listener quickly learns not to take outward appearances for granted. He discovers time and time again that people very seldom live up (or down) to first impressions.

At first glance, a self-assured posture may suggest a man with strength and confidence to spare. But sometimes, the posture is only a mask, and the person behind it is riddled with fears and feelings of inadequacy. In the initial stages of the laboratory experience, you may feel in awe of someone who seems to be highly intelligent, only to discover subsequently that you yourself have more practical knowledge at your fingertips.

Some people back away from the idea of "encounter groups"—another term for what we refer to as laboratory sessions—because they seem to think that the verbal interaction is all negative, that the sessions are largely devoted to pulling each other apart. This is a fallacy. The truth is that while a very valuable part of the experience is learning to recognize one's weak points and faults, an equally valuable knowledge can be acquired concerning strengths and talents of which one may be unaware.

Many people are held back by baseless feelings of inadequacy or inferiority. The laboratory group can point out hidden strengths and abilities. It can spotlight strengths you didn't think you had and alleviate groundless fears about one's ability to meet the challenges of one's professional or personal life. Here again, you have to accept the group's word as they see it. Nobody's going to earn any medals or promotions for praising you. You evaluate their observations.

Listening to the problems of others in the group may help you to erase traces of self-pity in your own makeup. A realization of how very un-unique one's worries are can free misdirected energies for better use. Many of us expect too much of ourselves. We aim at perfection, but we can't make it, so we castigate ourselves unfairly and deem our best efforts failures. This unrealistic behavior is as common as it is destructive. The lab teaches us that others are in the same boat. We're fond of saying, "Nobody's perfect," but we suspect that some people are—that there are perfect people somewhere who manage their lives without any of our hassles. It helps to know there aren't.

All human traits are shared to some extent by all human beings. A man or woman may blurt out a secret despair: "I'm so physically unattractive, people hate me!" This is an arrow that is bound to hit more than one other person in a circle of strangers. There just aren't that many beautiful people in the world.

Every man this side of Cary Grant and every woman this side of Liz Taylor has entertained doubts about some aspect—major or minor—of his or her appearance. So it's easy to reassure a person who thinks he is really unattractive. "You think you're homely—look at my nose!" Little by little, you can show that person that it isn't necessary to have matinee-idol features to be attractive, that real attractiveness comes from the heart. You may also be able to convince your ugly duckling that he is more attractive than he thinks he is. The big thing is, you can share and understand what he feels.

The range of human problems is enormous and their variety endless. Whatever your own particular hangup, it helps a lot to realize that you are not alone, you are never the only one—that no man *is* an island.

II. Let Your Ego Take Five

One day at a business luncheon, I found myself seated next to one of those men we've all met—the kind who ask you all about yourself but don't bother listening to the answers. Instead, they use your replies as springboards for talking about themselves. As soon as you say, "I'm a lawyer," or "I'm a salesman," they'll come back at you with a first-person spiel. My luncheon companion's was typical: "That's very interesting. I'm in the refrigerator game myself. Been in it twenty-five years. Regional manager. Started as an assembly worker back in 1945—no,

Let Your Ego Take Five

make that 1946, because I remember the war had just finished," and so forth and so on—I forget all the details of his very boring narrative.

One's self-esteem can really take a beating at the hands of such a person, because he obviously doesn't care who you are, what you do, or what makes you tick. So at this particular luncheon, I decided to have a little fun with this character, to make up the most outrageous story about myself I could think of and see what would happen. When he asked me what line I was in, I told him I was a zookeeper. When he asked me where I came from, I told him I was born in New Guinea and raised in French Guiana. When he asked me what I was doing at the luncheon, I told him I had just sneaked in for a free feed.

The man was incredible: My answers literally went in one ear and out the other. A zookeeper? "We have a real fine zoo in Cincinnati," was his reply. New Guinea? "I don't know much about that place, but I've been to Australia a couple of times. Heck of a country." Free feed? "Do it all the time, myself. I remember once when I was stranded in Houston . . ." and off he went again. The man had a serious case of I-itis.

Finally, I had had enough of him and his life story. I shook his hand briskly and said, "Well, Jones, it's been a real pleasure talking to you. Next time I'm in Wichita, I'll have to look you up. Maybe you'll sell me a television set at a discount." Dumfounded, he gaped at me. You see, his name was Hopkins, he was from Cincinnati, and he sold refrigerators.

The jokes about people not listening to each other are as old and as many as the hills:

In a reception line, a guest, answering the hostess's perfunctory greeting, murmurs, "I have leprosy."

"How perfectly wonderful! You must tell me all about it," trills the hostess, moving on to the next guest.

A housewife whose husband is buried in a televised football game will call out airily, "I'm going out to get some coffee and butter and a loaf of bread and a mink coat and some eggs, OK?"

"Sure, honey," comes the distracted reply, "Will you get me a carton of cigarettes while you're at it?"

And then there's the wife who sees no value in her husband's conversation other than as a springboard for her own. "Funny thing happened to me," the husband will say. "I got a call from this man who said he was . . ."

"Speaking of calls," interrupts his wife, "you'll never guess who called me today. Francine! After all this time. And guess what? She's pregnant, after trying for all these years."

We see the comic side of this common failing, and we go on laughing at what we have come to accept as a built-in human idiosyncrasy—one which we all share to some extent. But we pay less attention to the serious side of the matter. For the most part, we choose to ignore the fact that by not listening to each other we are reducing the possibility of mutual understanding in direct ratio to the number of messages we miss.

Often, by our tone of voice or enunciation, we try to tell somebody something we can't bring ourselves to say right out. We're saying one thing, but we mean something else, and we depend on the listener to sort it all out. Sometimes it works, sometimes it doesn't. It would be wonderful if we could all simply say what we mean 100 per cent of the time—but being mere mortals, we can't, and here's where the listener has to meet us halfway.

When we don't say exactly what we mean, three things can happen. The listener may catch the real, hidden message by listening carefully; he may choose to ignore it for reasons of his own (and he can always hold you to the fact that you said such-and-such); or he may innocently believe that you are saying what you mean and proceed on that assumption. In any case, you have only one out of three chances of gaining your true objective.

If we are to function more effectively—in our personal lives as well as in our business spheres—we must train ourselves to listen carefully. We must learn to listen to more than just the words that people say to us. We must train ourselves to "hear" the messages they are really trying to get across—to catch the unverbalized but nonetheless sincere meaning. We must learn to understand without explanations. We must stop taking words for granted.

Language needn't be complicated to befuddle the casual listener. Commonplace utterances can convey secret messages just as readily. The phrase "good morning," for example, is one we all hear many times each day. "Good morning" has got to be one of the most common, conventional phrases in our language—or for that matter, in any language. Taken literally, it expresses the wish that the person to whom the phrase is addressed may have a good morning (which presumably will pave the way for a good afternoon). Actually, it has lost all meaning. Most of us don't even take the trouble to take the phrase literally.

We just bounce "good mornings" off each other like tennis balls. It has become a conventional, automatic greeting—one that we hardly hear. But what happens if we break the pattern, if we listen carefully to all those "good mornings" bouncing off us as we walk into the office or make our way down Main Street? All kinds of messages begin to emerge, like invisible ink when moistened with lemon juice.

Let's start with the family circle. One "good morning" there tells you quite clearly that your mate is feeling disgustingly cheerful—or has a hangover, as the case may be; another announces that your eldest son is in a hell of a hurry to get somewhere; still another reveals that a younger daughter is hanging back, dreading the moment she must leave the house to go to school. Why the reluctance? Is she afraid of an examination, or is there something else that is worrying her? If you get the initial message, you can ask these questions and you stand a better chance of getting to the heart of her trouble before it can grow any more serious.

The range of hidden messages is just as wide at the office, where one can exchange as many "good mornings" as there are employees or employers in one's path. The office "good morning" can mean "Notice my new hairdo?" "I hope you drop dead," "What a lousy, rainy day!" "Late again, Harrison!" or "Gee, I'm glad you're my boss." Unfortunately, most of these little signals fly right past us without our ever giving them much notice.

Let Your Ego Take Five

The unheard office messages can be funny, too.
"Morning, Miss Jones, how are you today?"
"Awful."
"That's good. Will you bring your pad in, please? I have a letter I want to get out before noon."

The speaker obviously doesn't give a damn how Miss Jones feels, and he's so wound up in the thought of his own affairs, he doesn't even hear her reply. Naturally, Miss Jones is miffed at his lack of sympathy for whatever ails her, and she retaliates by making sure that the all-important letter gets out before noon, but only a few minutes before!

Choice of words and inflections in one's speech have a lot to do with sending out secret messages. "I guess so," or "I guess I can" fairly screams out, "I don't think so," or "I am very, very reluctant to do this." Just listen carefully the next time your secretary or an elevator operator or a waiter calls you "sir." It's fantastic how much feeling a person can fit into that one little one-syllable word. The emotion can range all the way from out-and-out adoration to cool disdain or smoldering hatred.

Any way you look at it, you're bound to benefit by listening more carefully. Whose day isn't made a little brighter by a moderate dose of adoration? And if it's disdain or worse you hear, you can be sure you're doing something wrong. There's something about your behavior that bugs that particular person, and if you're the average person with the average person's concern for others, you'll try to figure out what it is and make amends. It may not be of earth-shaking importance, but it will just help to make everybody's day run a little smoother.

Sad but true, most of us hear what we want to hear and block out the rest, whether it's implied criticism or simply something that we consider irrelevant—irrelevant in this case meaning something that doesn't engage our direct attention. It's a common form of single-mindedness.

We are so keen on achieving our own ends, we tend to discount any point of view that might possibly get in the way. We can't bear the notion that anything or anybody might block acceptance of our own point of view. Does anybody with an idea on any subject take kindly to the possibility that the person sitting across the luncheon or conference table may have an even better idea on the same subject? Of course not. Yet, if the two men put their egos aside and really listened to each other, they might be able to put their two ideas together and come up with a truly inspiring third idea.

Listening is learning, and by learning to listen, we open doors to wider knowledge, increased wisdom and, inevitably, a greater understanding of ourselves and those around us.

The ego can be a very effective earplug. A frighteningly high percentage of normal conversations are not true conversations at all. They're just two people talking at each other, each one giving far more thought to what he's going to say next than he is giving to what the other fellow is saying. It's like two people taking turns talking to themselves out loud.

How many times have you caught the tail end of another person's sentence and sensed that you've missed something really interesting, yet been too embarrassed to admit that you didn't hear the first part of the sentence? It's all but impossible to admit that you haven't been paying attention to what somebody says when you've been sitting right in front of him, making an effort to look as though you're listening, although your thoughts are actually miles away. This sort of thing can't be called a conversation. It's an exercise in futility.

Listening is the first link in the chain of communication that links people together. Non-listening can lead to non-relationships or worse, misunderstandings and unwarranted antagonisms that prevent people from coming together. If you want to see how this works, try a simple experiment:

Think of somebody—a sister-in-law, a co-worker, an aged relative—to whom you habitually turn half an ear or none. It has to be a person—and there's bound to be at least one in your life—whom you consider a bore, whose conversation you almost automatically tune out. The next time you find yourself caught in a conversation with this person, let your ego take five and really concentrate on listening to what he or she has to say. Pay attention, and ask questions if you have to.

You'll be surprised—no, amazed—to find out how much more willing you'll be and how much easier it will be to accept this person, conversational warts and all, once you have listened to what he or she has to say. I'm not saying the person you thought was such a bore will suddenly turn out to be a fascinating raconteur. That only happens in fiction or the movies. But you will have removed a stumbling block to mutual understanding. You cannot help but learn something from listening to that person, because the simple fact is that there are few really true-blue, 100 per cent bores in this world. We all have something interesting to say about something—more and less interesting sides to our personalities. By not paying attention or by listening haphazardly, we stand a good chance of catching only a dull aspect of a person's nature and never come to realize how interesting he or she can be.

Sometimes, we go further than just plain not listening. We prevent communication. You know how it is when you're trying to talk with someone who isn't paying any attention to what you're saying. What happens? You stop trying, right? Well, this works the other way around as well. When we flaunt our own lack of interest in front of another person, we commit that person to silence, we create an atmosphere of non-communication. We couldn't do it any more effectively if we turned to the person and said, "Will you please shut up? I'm not interested in a word you have to say."

Later, we are all self-righteousness. "I couldn't get him to say a word," we'll announce, although the truth is more likely that we didn't try very hard to encourage a word. The true fault lies in our own unwillingness to listen or to display a minimal degree of interest.

At a party in London, I ran into an American business friend of mine who was accompanied by his wife—a very beautiful woman whose vanity overshadowed her obvious intelligence. The occasion was a reception given by a publisher, and the guest list was impressive and varied. As the party progressed, I noticed the wife of my friend across the room, standing next to a slight, trim, but rather unprepossessing-looking gentleman. They weren't talking to each other. He was looking rather uncomfortable, and she was scanning the room, smiling absently at other guests. She looked for all the world like a girl at a college dance, signaling the stag line to be rescued from her clumsy partner.

Later, I asked her what she had thought of the unprepossessing-looking gentleman. "What a dreadful bore," she explained. "I thought I would never be rid of him!" I smiled to myself, but I couldn't bring myself to tell her that the man she thought was such an enormous bore, whose name meant nothing to her (probably, she didn't even hear it when he introduced himself), had won the Nobel Prize for Chemistry the year before. Surely, he must have had something interesting to say, if only she had been interested enough to encourage him to say it.

What are human relationships, really? When we boil them down, they are a form of dialogue. Without dialogue, people would lapse into autistic trances, focusing totally inward and trapped forever in the cages of their own identities. But it's other people who help give us our sense of identity, and only through dialogue can identity be fully established.

But dialogue doesn't mean both parties talking at once; it means one communicating and one receiving— one pitching and one catching, then one catching and the other pitching alternately. When it's your turn to catch, you listen. But listening isn't a passive process, as is commonly thought. Like a good baseball catcher, the good listener flashes signals and the speaker tries to follow them. The good listener says, "This is what I want you to tell me, this is what I need to know to help me understand you and get along with you."

Every successful pitcher will admit that it's only because he has a good catcher that he's winning most of his games. But too many people think all the glory goes to the pitcher; likewise, people are more eager to speak than listen because they figure that most of the glory belongs to the speaker. Such people are so eager to pitch that they become lousy catchers. The dialogue is destroyed, and the ballgame is lost.

At best this makes for frustration, at worst it can be terribly destructive, like a wife I heard about who walked out on her husband after ten years of trying to get him to listen to her. It was not just what she was saying with her lips, but what she was trying to convey with her heart. He was totally shocked when she left him and to this day he doesn't understand what happened. What happened was, he had given her no emotional responses, no signals of appreciation or understanding or care. Slowly the dialogue had dried up.

But the last communication belonged to her: "So long, buddy."

If not listening carefully is a common fault and one of the principal obstacles to communication and understanding, so is its opposite—an equally common social affliction which could be called the Small Talk Syndrome. It reaches epidemic proportions at cocktail parties, but it can also be encountered in the home, at a board table, or in the lounge of a 747. Here, instead of indifference, a torrent of small talk blocks communicative channels.

There are those people who think that any space occupied by more than one person has to be continually filled with the sound of running chatter. They believe that silence or even a long pause in a conversation immediately signifies some kind of social (or business) failure. These people keep on talking as if their lives depended on it. They even go so far as to pride themselves on what they consider their ability to "keep the conversation moving."

What these people fail to realize is that their constant chatter doesn't really help to move the conversation in any meaningful direction. They're just keeping a lot of words in the air, as a juggler juggles plates or Indian clubs. More important, how can these people ever manage to listen to anybody else? The answer is, they don't. They think that they can create a "conversation" all by themselves. They contribute little, and they learn less. As a result of their garrulousness, they stunt their mental growth by locking themselves into boxes of knowledge—usually pretty scanty knowledge, at that—which cannot expand in any direction.

With so many sets of adverse circumstances to contend with, it is no wonder that one can rarely find a perfect setting for perfect communication with others in one's everyday life. All systems are almost never "go." But the behavioral science laboratory has managed to overcome the ordinary obstacles one encounters, to create a climate for total listening. This climate is as necessary to the successful laboratory session as a roof over its head or oxygen in the air.

Just think of it—ten people, sitting around in a circle, forced to talk about themselves and each other. No member of the group can avoid listening. Even if he tries to, the group will force itself into his hearing. And conversely, nobody can avoid contributing to the verbal exchange. Anybody who remains silent for long will be challenged to give his views by the rest.

Perhaps the number one lesson of the lab is how to listen. A police inspector from Detroit told me that this was the most important lesson he learned while attending a week-long session, and others have echoed this view. In the case of the policeman, now he can more easily "hear" the person behind the beard and the beads because he has learned to sidestep his preconceived ideas and really listen to what that person has to say. A man sporting a dashiki and an afro hairdo has a better chance than he had before of getting his message past these obvious symbols of his racial identity.

It works the other way around, too. A student who participated in one of our labs became particularly friendly with an older man, who turned out to be a policeman. During one session, the policeman explained to the group his fears of failing in his chosen profession, his deep concern that he might not be able to reach the goals he had set for himself. When, toward the end of the session, the members of the group bared their identities to each other, the student, who had listened carefully to the policeman's story, found it easier to discard his automatic antipathy toward the police, which he was compelled to admit was based mostly on fear. He'd never really talked with a policeman before.

While the laboratory experience can teach people to listen, an individual trying to teach the same lesson has a harder time, as any parent can testify. "Now you listen to me!" Has anybody ever said that to you? And what happened when they did? Chances are that you responded by turning your thoughts as far away as they would go—to how the fishing would be for the weekend, or why anybody ever painted that wall that particular shade of green. The phrase is a very poor imperative. It practically guarantees that the person to whom it is addressed will "tune out" immediately. The laboratory experience brings this perverse phrase to life by making it happen.

Why is it that people don't listen to each other in ordinary circumstances? In some cases, they're probably afraid of what they might hear. A man who knows he's slipping in his work isn't going to listen readily to criticism, however diplomatically it may be proffered. He's afraid. He has to pretend to himself that everything is just fine and dandy.

But most of the time, our not listening stems from just plain carelessness or lack of interest. We're too busy rushing on to the next thing. We think we don't have time to listen to somebody else because we're too wrapped up in ourselves, we're too involved in what we're doing. In the laboratory setting, there's plenty of time for everything but navel-gazing. There you are, there is nothing to do but listen, and you're stuck with what you hear. The opportunity for learning is unequaled, because the fact that there are nine other people participating in the verbal interaction means that you can suddenly, magically, raise your own listening quotient to the power of ten.

Increased listening power can help you to lead a fuller life in very many ways. But just to take a pragmatic view—think of the business opportunities that are lost by lack of listening! Think of the loss of talent and ideas! An office manager may ask a drooping clerk, "What's the matter?" And the clerk, whose wife has just left him and whose doctor has informed him that he needs an immediate, serious operation, answers glumly, "Nothing."

A careful listener will simply not let the conversation end on that note. If he really wants to hear the true answer to his question, he'll hang in there until he gets it. He'll insist on knowing what the matter really is. But an inadequate listener (who, as a matter of course, must also be an inadequate manager) will sidestep the problem, neatly accepting "Nothing" as the true answer even although he is aware that it isn't. He can't be bothered. He's not interested in the clerk's troubles, he's got woes of his own.

Of course, as anybody who has read the best-selling book *Body Language* or any of the dozens of magazine articles it inspired knows, words are not the only tools of communication we possess. Besides words—and the words behind words—we must learn to interpret the messages people send in looks and gestures and nervous mannerisms. The direction of one's gaze, or a toe tapping nervously can relay a message all its own. No matter how calm his facial expression is or how confidently he speaks, a man who is fidgeting with his fingers or running his hand through his hair at frequent intervals is not at ease. His gestures belie any verbal expressions of confidence. They tell you that much. And if you manage to understand that message, you can press for reasons—if you're interested and really care to hear them.

Lawrence Spivak, the sharp-witted mentor of the fabulously successful television show "Meet the Press," has praised the use of television for political debates. He has claimed that the television eye bares the phony, however glibly he presents his case; and likewise, it reveals the sincerity of another speaker, even though he may stumble badly over his words. How is this possible? Obviously, the words and the way in which they are delivered add up to only one half of the whole message. The rest of the message is transmitted by gestures and bearing and received in one's conscious or subconscious reaction to the person who is speaking. For we reveal our true selves in every intonation of our voices, in every movement that we make.

In one of our laboratory sessions, a man's managerial shortcomings gradually became apparent to the rest of the group. It was a delicate, but not a particularly unusual situation. The man had been promoted over a former superior, and he was having a great deal of trouble asserting his authority in his new post. As the group caught on to this fact, the man was barraged with questions. Why did he let the old guy get away with so much? Why didn't he make use of his new authority? At first, the group pleaded, then it forced the man to listen to what it had to say. Although he was unable to respond verbally, the man's reaction to the barrage was obvious.

Wetting his lips nervously, he tried to light a cigarette, but his hands wouldn't co-operate. They were shaking too hard for him too accomplish this simple feat without difficulty. It was only much later that he arrived at the point where he could express his understanding and acceptance of the group's opinions verbally. He admitted he'd been allowing his former boss to get away with murder, and he acknowledged that this course of action or inaction had seriously undermined the morale and effectiveness of his department. With the help of the group's observations, he could also not help but see that he had acted in this manner out of residual fear and misplaced "respect" (which was really a kind of pity) for his former superior.

Who listens, learns. It's as simple as that. You can sit through the most fascinating lecture on the most fascinating subject in the world—whatever that may be—and if you don't pay attention to what is being said, you might as well be sitting in the park feeding the pigeons. It's the same thing with interpersonal relationships. If we are to understand other people and through them, ourselves, we must listen to what they have to say.

If the obvious advantages of this argument don't completely convince you, think about this: Other people probably don't hear half of what you say to them when you seek to express your views on a certain subject. Don't you think this means they're missing something?

Perhaps a variation of the Golden Rule might serve as an effective reminder to lend a whole ear to the other fellow: Listen to others as you would have others listen to you.

III. How to Succeed in Business Without Really Lying

Is honesty the best policy? Is it possible to succeed in business without really lying?

The chairman of the board of a large insurance company attended a laboratory session in Ann Arbor. His participation was steady, but cautious. He was obviously making an effort, but something was wrong. Suddenly, on the third day of the session, a young man half his age blew up at him.

"Goddammit," he yelled, "you haven't told the truth for four days! Why don't you get off your high horse and give us some straight talk?" Stunned by the accusation and armed with this unexpected view of himself as others saw him, the man took a new tack and opened up to the group. Ultimately, he came to the realization that during his long climb to the top of his company, he had gradually insulated himself more and more from honest feedback. He had become accustomed to the lies of his subordinates and had even come to accept second-guessing as part of his managerial role.

The man's plight was not an unusual one by any means. For the sad truth about the truth is that its natural course is downward, rather than upward. The guys at the top are free to tell the truth with impunity, but the guys at the bottom often keep their mouths shut—or even lie—because they are afraid their honesty might earn them a demotion or something worse.

Not long ago, Doyle Dane Bernback, the well-known New York advertising firm, contributed a one-page ad for a series of advertisements on the subject of advertising, sponsored by *Time* magazine. "I got a great gimmick," the headline announced. "Let's tell the truth." The copy went on to illustrate the money-making advantages of telling the truth and to point out practical reasons for doing so.

In the ad, the agency described its first client as the man who claimed that the truth would make a great advertising gimmick. Well, maybe twenty years ago, the truth was a novelty in advertising—something the average consumer didn't expect to find. The advertising world had earned itself an international reputation for across-the-board chicanery in novels like *The Hucksters*. But we are hopeful that as both ad agencies and consumers have gained in wisdom, thanks to the media explosion, the truth is coming into its own as a way of getting one's message across. As the *Time* ad put it, "People are as smart as we are. That's why we tell the truth." No moralizing—no little sermons for little people. The truth works.

The truth also pays—sometimes, in unexpected ways. When the truth is unpleasant, people sometimes tell it because they feel they have to, and they expect no rewards. The common expression is, "I guess I'll have to face the music"—but occasionally, the music turns out to be sweeter than one had hoped or expected.

A small boiler manufacturer in Pennsylvania enjoyed a modest degree of success for many years. Then the man who founded the company died, and his son, who succeeded him, began to look for new ways to increase the company's profits. He put in a bid for a contract with one of the largest corporations in the country.

His plant's bid turned out to be the lowest, and the firm got the contract. As the final stages of production were reached, an engineer in the plant noticed that to gain time, the workmen had been cutting corners on welds. He went to the young president of the firm to report this and to warn that the boilers would not be safe if they were allowed to be shipped out in their present state. Repairing the welds would take several weeks, carrying the company well over the deadline for delivery. It would also raise production costs substantially.

After considering all factors, the young president made

a crucial decision. He went to see the vice-president in charge of purchasing for the large corporation (on whom, by now, the future of the smaller company depended). He told the vice-president the whole truth, concluding with the declaration that if the corporation still wanted its boilers, it would have to wait a few more weeks. And if it wanted them guaranteed safe, it would have to make an adjustment in the original contract to meet the unexpected cost overrun.

The large corporation could easily have canceled its contract, and nobody in the hard, cold world of business would have faulted that decision. But the corporation's vice-president was impressed by the younger businessman's courage in taking the blame for the delay and explaining the causes of the trouble so honestly. He agreed to renegotiate the contract for a slightly higher figure and to allow time for the faulty welds to be repaired.

It might certainly have been easier for the young manufacturer to ship the boilers and run, and to disclaim all responsibility if one of the boilers blew up or failed. But he chose to level with his customer, so the story had a happy ending. The truth of the matter is, people are impressed by honesty!

It's strange when you think about it. Honesty is one of the first lessons we are taught as children and one of the first we are taught to forget as we enter what adults are fond of calling "the real world." A child hears the story of George Washington and the cherry tree with innocent, envy-tinged admiration for Washington's courage. The grown man, wise to the ways of the world, reflects on the story and sums George Washington up as a patsy. The man may feel what the child has no way of knowing—that one can occasionally be punished for telling the truth. But punishing the truthful makes them into liars.

One of the most important benefits of the laboratory experience is that it forces participants to recognize the value of the truth. In the behavioral science laboratory, everybody starts out equal with everybody else. Each participant begins the session with his old, bad habits in fine working order.

At an ABS session one winter, a big-time executive, champing inwardly at the initial silence of the group, blurted out, "I've got five thousand men working under me! I don't need this, and I'm not going to waste any more time here!" But before he could actually take his leave, the shock of his words acted like a catalyst on the group and as the verbal exchange began, the power of the group dynamic took hold and before Mr. Bigshot knew what was happening to him, he was up to his neck in the exciting process of self-discovery—acquiring as he went along a new awareness of other people as represented by the other participants in the session.

During the laboratory experience, the true traits of a person have the best chance they will ever have of coming to the surface. Nobody has to be polite, as a friend or co-worker might feel compelled to be, so empty compliments and false modesty go out the window. As you learn from the group just exactly how your behavior hits them, you find out what makes you tick. You may even gain insights into areas of your personality and behavior that you've either been too busy to notice or unwilling to accept before. Most of us are unaware of how we appear to others.

In your rush to get ahead or to reach a goal you have set for yourself, you may have ignored everyone around you and earned yourself a reputation as a crotchety hermit type. But you can't see this all by yourself. It's like being too close to the forest to see the trees.

A large public utility corporation in New York State had what it thought was a bright idea. The management initiated a point system to monitor the effectiveness of the corporation's over-all operation. Human beings being what they are, the result was predictable.

Quite naturally, department heads were reluctant to admit that their people might not be pulling their weight. To put it politely, they exaggerated their subordinates' performances in their regular reports. "My people are operating at 10 per cent above the average production level for our department," a typical report would state—when the truth was, production was falling off sharply, and those same subordinates were not even managing to meet their minimum quotas.

As a result of this self-protective deception, the men at the top, who had initiated the system to discover where problems might be lurking, had absolutely no idea of what was really going on at the lower levels of their operation, and several of the company's minor inefficiencies blossomed into a public scandal and pages and pages of bad publicity for the corporation before the truth was discovered and the situation could be reversed.

Honesty, like charity, has to begin at home. The individual must learn to be honest with himself before he can succeed at being honest with the rest of the world. The more we discover about ourselves, the more useful we can be, and the simpler it is to find direct solutions to our personal and business problems. Free from self-deception, a man is free to improve himself. In fact, it is only when he can see what is wrong with his behavior that he is in a position to change or modify it to his own advantage.

A famous movie star of my acquaintance was well past his prime when I first met him in the late 1950s. He was obviously hovering on the brink of a complete breakdown. He hadn't worked for three years, and he couldn't face the fact that his magnificent career as a matinee idol was on the rocks. His house in Beverly Hills was lined with photographs, awards, and other mementos of his heyday. Visiting the place was like visiting a museum.

The root of the problem was clearly visible to everybody but the actor himself. The real trouble was that his agent—well aware of the effect the truth would have on his client's tender and considerable ego, kept assuring him he was as handsome and virile-looking as ever. He compounded this error by continuing to propose his client for romantic leads—again, largely out of consideration for the actor's feelings. Of course, the actor was growing too old—visibly too old—for that kind of role, and no producer was willing to hire him for one. Occasionally, a producer would offer the agent a character part for his client, but this was something the agent thought it best to keep to himself.

Finally in desperation, the agent leveled with the actor. He told him bluntly that he was over the hill as far as romance was concerned, but he softened the blow by reminding the fading star that his talent was still there, and if he wanted to, he could still score a considerable success in character roles.

The actor's first reaction to this information was to fire his agent and retreat even further into the folds of his past. But after a few weeks of thinking it over, he recovered from the shock and telephoned the agent to apologize and thank him for telling the truth. By readjusting his thinking along with his film image, the actor is now enjoying a whole new career in the twilight of his life. The only irony is that this second career could have started three years earlier if the agent had known how to make constructive use of the truth, and if the actor had been prepared to accept it at that time.

Nobody is about to suggest that if large numbers of citizens woke up on a given morning constitutionally unable to tell a lie, all problems would be solved. The truth-givers must be matched by an equal number of truth-receivers at all levels. Most important, those in a position to deal out punishments must learn to accept the truth as an honest, fair and valuable form of communication. This attitude will encourage people in minor positions of authority to be more truthful in their attitudes toward their superiors.

It is also important to remember that honesty must not be carried to the point of stupidity, or itself employed as a tool of revenge or counter-punishment. One must be prepared to decide when the truth is necessary to the improvement of a situation or a relationship, and when it will serve no useful purpose, but will only hurt or cause harm.

This important distinction is contantly being made in our laboratory sessions. A good trainer (or facilitator, as some prefer to call our group leaders) can quickly detect the point where honest criticism crosses the line and becomes sadistic browbeating. Putting a stop to the abuse, the trainer can then try to ascertain why the person who dished it out was prompted to go so far—and equally important, why the person who bore the brunt of the attack in silence allowed the other person to humiliate him so.

A vital distinction must be made between the kind of honesty I've been preaching and the garden variety social fib. We're taught as youngsters that "white lies" are often okay. We all agree that it is all right—sometimes, even necessary—to lie about your hostess's new, blue hairdo, or your host's second-rate whiskey. That kind of lying comes under the heading of Not Hurting Other Peoples' Feelings, and it's a perfectly acceptable social convention. But it cannot be transferred intact to the business world without wreaking a lot of damage.

In corporate life, lies can cost money, time, jobs. In a business situation, the truth may hurt some feelings, but if left untold, it can wind up doing far more extensive damage.

A man I know—I'll call him Mr. B.—retired about seven years before he planned to because nobody told him the truth when it came time to make a vital decision. As executive vice-president of a company manufacturing small electrical appliances, B. was in charge of new products.

Shared Participation

On his own, B. had developed a revolutionary new design for an appliance—for my lawyers' sake we'll call it a gizmo. Before putting it into production, B. sought the advice of key members of his engineering staff. Aware of his pride in his design, the engineers told B. it was the best-looking, best-performing gizmo they had ever seen. In fact, it was flawed. Its functional quality had been sacrificed for the sake of greater aesthetic appeal, but as B. had a way of promoting those people around him who filled his day with "yeses," nobody had the guts to point out the gizmo's faults, and the thing went on the market.

It looked like a million, and it sold like hotcakes. But within six weeks, most of the gizmos had been returned to the retailers who sold them. The corporation almost lost its shirt, and B. retired several years ahead of schedule. How much better it would have been for all concerned if some brave soul had simply informed the vice-president.

How much smoother the path to profit would be if honesty were treasured as highly as punctuality in a manufacturing plant! Practically every other week, we read in the newspapers about an automotive firm recalling tens of thousands of models for defective brakes or some other mechanical infirmity. Is it possible that nobody in those vast plants recognized the defects on the assembly line or test track—or even earlier, on the drawing board? Or isn't it likelier that a foreman or inspector decided that nobody in management was going to hand him a medal for raising a problem that would

How to Succeed ... Without Lying

send production costs soaring to remedy? This action is called Sticking Your Neck Out, and not many people do it any more. So the cars go out defective, risking bodily injury to their drivers and passengers, and then have to be publicly recalled—providing the firm with a lot of free, adverse publicity, not to mention customer inconvenience, loss of sales, and potential lawsuits.

The mention of automobiles brings to mind an example of honesty in advertising which is close to my heart—the "We're Number Two" campaign launched some years ago on behalf of the car rental agency that bears my name. Doyle, Dane, Bernbach figured in this campaign, too, but interestingly enough, it wasn't until after I'd sold my interest in the company that its directors turned to DDB and asked them for ideas on the best promotional approach to take in the hotly competitive car-rental market. The agency analyzed Avis' situation and concluded that the only way to promote it was to come on honestly and declare that Avis was only the second-largest car rental agency—but it tried harder!

The campaign transformed Avis from a well-known corporation into a household word. The basis of the campaign? No magic formula—just the truth. What an unbeatable sales pitch!

Our society makes a practice of punishing people for telling the truth, even when it's asked for. We may punish a subordinate with angry silence or something worse if he gives an honest, unflattering opinion of a speech or report we have written. On a personal level, one may ask a good friend, "Do you think I'm too fat?" And the friend, being a good friend, tells the truth. "Well, you do seem to be getting a little paunchy, now that you mention it." Do not ask for the truth unless you want it.

This sort of thing cannot happen in the laboratory, where everybody is a stranger to everybody else. There are no friendships to be fractured, no recourses to turned-down promotions and other measures of official revenge, no hurt feelings cutting into a hitherto warm relationship. Nobody has anything to lose, and everybody has much to gain by being truthful.

Any man or woman who goes through the laboratory experience will become more truthful as a matter of course. He or she will have gained new insights into his reactions and developed a keener awareness of the effect his behavior has on other people. This person is, therefore, in a far better position to cope with managerial problems than the traditional executive figure, remote and insulated from self-awareness by the silence or rote praise of his subordinates.

The fact of the matter is that in a laboratory you can't get away with lies. Nowhere is Lincoln's dictum that "You can't fool all of the people all of the time" more in evidence than here, for there's always one person in the circle at least who has your number, whose ears are attuned to a certain pitch you give off and can detect a false note at once.

Although their functions are quite different, a lab and a jury have something in common. Both are trying to get at the truth, and both are founded on the principle that a small group of ordinary people is likelier to learn the truth than a single individual no matter how extraordinary. For, every person has at least one serious fault which blinds him to certain truths—he either can't see them or won't. The most learned magistrate may overlook an important fact when the accused is brought before him, or a brilliant psychiatrist when a patient tells his story, because some flaw in their personalities predisposes them to do so. In a lab, as in a jury, such errors are minimized.

Sir Walter Scott was right. Continuous, habitual half-truths and lies of convenience lead us into a very tangled web. They also waste a lot of precious, irreplaceable time.

In business affairs, we become conditioned to what might euphemistically be termed "managerial misstatement." We worry a lot about what would happen if the truth were known. What if our competitor found out about the new model? What if our customers discovered the true facts about our margin of profit? Confused and ensnared in our own webs of deceit, we are led into the reasonable, but fatal notion that everybody else must be lying, too. As a result, we spend an inordinate amount of time during business discussions trying to figure out what Mr. X. really means when he says production costs will rise 2 per cent over the next two years. Does he mean they'll rise 5 per cent, or perhaps that they won't rise at all? Sooner or later, we lose the ability to spot the truth when it is told to us, and so its value is nullified. When we lose trust, we lose time.

On the other hand, in business life as in one's personal life, there are many rewards to be reaped by the simple telling of the truth. Aside from the heady feeling of virtue it imparts, it is just plain easier to tell the truth than it is to lie.

One of the commonest corporate lies, sometimes called Passing the Buck, is the practice of lying to avoid blame for a major or minor goof. This may involve several different lies in several different directions; and remembering which story was told to which person can take a lot of time and concentration—both of which could be put to better uses for the company than saving one's own skin. This practice could be avoided entirely if honesty were encouraged or at least tolerated by men at the top. They should realize that it is the incompetent who must lie to temporarily save his job.

We are gradually developing into a dishonest society. We indifferently accept lies as "life" and do nothing in particular to promote honesty. This failure to act in behalf of honesty can be fatal, for a dishonest society cannot survive—and more importantly on a day-to-day pragmatic level, it really does not pay. This can be seen at the highest levels of national affairs.

The mad scramble for budgetary dollars in the United States Congress has created a veritable network of half-truths and lies around the Capitol itself—a whole class of lobbyists whose chief weapon of persuasion is systematized exaggeration. It is part of the accepted routine for these lobbyists to request two or three times the amount they really need, because they know that by the time the appropriations committees are through with their deliberations, they can consider themselves fortunate to get a whittled-down fraction of the amount they requested, which often represents the amount that was required in the first place. Like a cat chasing its own tail, this deceitful practice breeds more deceit and excludes the possibility of truly honest lobbying. Pity the poor, uninitiated lobbyist who asked for exactly the amount he needed! The legislators, hardened to exaggerated demands and the current system of give-and-take, would automatically cut the figure down. They couldn't be expected, on their own, to recognize the difference between an honest, uninflated request and the run-of-the-mill petition.

In the arena of international affairs, the effects of dishonesty are even more alarming. There was a time when the ritual, diplomatic lie was hardly more than a polished veneer to insure cordial and courteous relations between diplomats. But today, the face-saving propaganda that has grown out of this old, polite practice has become a perilous exercise in brinksmanship, as nuclear powers, exaggerating the capacities of their destructive arsenals, force competitors and potential enemies into dangerous arms escalations. Nobody seems ready to call it quits—to confess he has fewer arms or is just plain frightened. The end result of all this my-dad-can-beat-your-dad thinking at top international levels is just too horrible to contemplate. An honest, straightforward approach to common understanding is the only viable alternative we have.

Society must learn how to use honesty constructively. If any two people with differences could sit down and talk them out honestly, accepting each other's frankness in a positive way, they might solve their mutual problem

—or at least reach a workable compromise. The same thing applies to society in general.

All organizations should seek out honest men, not yes-men. The result—a vastly improved system of communication between people and peoples—can't help but lead to better people, better business, and—perhaps for the first time in the history of a battered planet—lasting peace.

IV. Shared Participation

Everybody in this world is "them" to somebody else. If you're a corporate executive, you're "them" to the union people in your company; if you're a blue-collar worker, or even a low-echelon white-collar worker, you're "them" to the guys in the executive suites; parents are "them" to children and vice versa; and so it goes. We'd be well on our way to better lives and a better society if we could band together to turn all our "them"s into one big "we." Through ignorance, we are setting up a conflict society instead of a problem-solving society.

Togetherness is an inherent tradition of the human

race. Cave men huddled together for warmth and mutual protection, and we tend to do the same today. It's a theme that appeals to everyone. The contemporary slang expression, "getting yourself together" implies a certain mental order, a healthy way of looking at things and an enviable state of satisfaction with one's self. There's a joy in sharing, in doing things together.

Unfortunately, in our modern society, many of us find ourselves really pulling together only in emergencies—when a natural calamity occurs or there's a transportation strike in a metropolitan area. The rest of the time, we have developed a tendency to go it alone, to look after ourselves as best we can and let the other guy take care of himself in the same way. It would be better for everybody and everything if we could learn to pool our resources and work together toward common goals in everyday life, instead of just when a calamity strikes.

At ABS, we've evolved a decision-making system which we feel is an important step in this direction. It is geared to the notion of involving a wide range of diverse talents to deal with any given problem. It's called Shared Participation, and it is our way of turning "them" into "we."

Shared Participation is just what the name implies—a system of pulling all the "thems" together into a multi-experienced group that can operate as a cohesive, comprehensive decision-making task force. As the saying goes, "The more, the merrier!" Our version is, "The more, the better!" If two heads working together under a proper structure are better than one, why not put ten, twenty,

Shared Participation

or fifty together? This obviously can be done only in an atmosphere of trust where individual ego needs do not dominate.

Maier won fame for his formula: The effectiveness of a decision equals the quality of a decision times the acceptance of a decision. In other words, if you've got a perfectly great decision, but nobody is willing to accept it, it's not as great as you thought it was. Its effectiveness is reduced by at least half. Maier further defined the quality of a decision as equaling the judgment that went into its making.

As far as it went, it was fine, but it set me wondering: What do we mean by the word "judgment"? It's a perfectly ordinary, much-used word. It's also a weighty word—one that effects the total quality of our lives. But it's also hard to pin down, and the dictionary definitions just scratch its surface. After a good deal of consideration, I came up with a formula that seemed to supply the fuller explanation I was seeking:

$$Judgment = Knowledge + Experience$$

To make the definition even more precise, I added the word "Intuition," for it seemed to me that Knowledge and Experience did not sufficiently include this elusive but vital innate human power. The revised formula reads as follows:

$$Judgment = Knowledge + Experience + Intuition$$

I still wasn't completely satisfied. The first three elements of my formula seemed clear enough, but the new addition seemed to require a definition of its own. To clarify this point, I added a subdefinition for Intuition, which I decided, like ancient Gaul, was divided into three parts: subconscious knowledge and experience; heredity; and creativity. It also occurred to me that that good old Yankee term "know how" would be an apt alternative definition for "Knowledge+Experience." My formula was beginning to look like *War and Peace*, but it finally said exactly what I was trying to express:

$$\text{Judgment} = \underset{(\text{Know How})}{\text{Knowledge} + \text{Experience}} + \text{Intuition} \genfrac{}{}{0pt}{}{\nearrow \ \ \substack{\text{Subconscious Knowledge} \\ +\text{Experience} \\ \text{Heredity}}}{\searrow \ \ \text{Creativity}}$$

Having completed my formula, I returned to the problem of making good decisions.

It is perfectly apparent to anybody who habitually has to do it that decision-making is a fine art. The right path to take or the appropriate course of action is seldom obvious to us. In most cases, it takes a good deal of weighing, pondering and comparing to make up one's mind; and the time it takes to make a decision depends on the number of factors to be weighed and pondered, as well as the number of comparisons that are available to us as points of reference. Approximately 80 per cent of all judgment decisions are made through the application of knowledge and experience. The other 20 per cent are made by using one's intuition. But at least 50 per cent of all intuition is subconscious knowledge and experience. The other 50 per cent is heredity, over which we have no control. The other factor in intuition is creativity which produces new combinations beyond existing knowledge and experience.

Shared Participation is a system which guarantees the best possible decision in every case to which it is applied. Why? Because the decision-making process in Shared Participation involves the widest possible range of knowledge and experience. The resultant decision is a decision by consensus. A wide range of people involved in the decision, whose lives will be affected by it in the end, are asked to make it. This system insures both prerequisites for a good decision. Not only do you wind up with a real corker of an answer to your problem, but it also follows quite naturally that this kind of multiple decision will enjoy maximum acceptance as a built-in bonus. Nobody tends to carp about a decision he's had a voice in.

In addition to serving as a boon for its participants in terms of morale and decision quality, the Shared Participation system also provides an easy method of tapping priceless human resources which are wasted under conventional management systems. It extends the sphere of influence to the widest degree and brings the greatest amount of knowledge, experience, and creativity to bear on a given problem. In a sense it constitutes a modernization of the old-fashioned "suggestion box." As a replacement, it is certainly timely. The suggestion box is sadly out of date in the electronic age. It often represented only an empty gesture on the part of management. Besides, it had the built-in disadvantage of attracting solutions that were the result of only one person's knowledge and experience—and the wisest man has many limitations when it comes to facing a particular problem. Few individuals have the ability to consider all sides of a problem equally in seeking to find its solution. Shared Participation is a way of pooling the best ideas available on every aspect of the problem and boiling them down, so to speak, to produce the best possible judgment or answer to that problem.

One advantage which the Shared Participation system shares with the suggestion box from the employees' point of view is that it conceals the identity of individual participants in order to provide a climate of absolute freedom and an unrestricted flow of ideas and suggestions. Shared Participation is a team effort in every sense of the word.

This is how Shared Participation works. The process begins with management selecting a number of workers to be grouped into ten-man teams. The number of teams depends on the size of the company or even the size of the problem to be examined by the teams. As many departments as are involved or will be affected by the problem should, naturally, be represented on the decision-making team. This means you might have anywhere from ten to fifty people participating in a single Shared Participation program.

It is very important that each individual team be composed of co-workers of nearly equal status. For example, you might have three ten-man teams: two composed of production employees, and one made up of foremen and supervisors. The reasons for this are fairly obvious. Everybody feels more comfortable with his peers; and production line workers, for example, can talk freely among themselves, whereas they might feel constricted or inhibited by the presence of a "boss" figure in their midst.

The first step in the Shared Participation process is called Data Collecting. All the ten-man teams are assembled, and management explains whatever it is that has to be explained, whatever problem is due to be taken under consideration. It could be anything—a breakdown in interdepartmental communications, quality control, or something as general as how to improve the company's over-all efficiency and production.

The second step of the Data Collecting phase of the operation begins as the ten-man teams subdivide themselves into five-man subteams. Now, every participant is given a piece of paper and instructed to write down five ideas—the five most important things he can think of which he feels might contribute to the ultimate solution of the problem at hand. As soon as this is accomplished, these ideas are collected and consolidated into one longer list, so that each five-man subteam winds up with a "master" list of twenty-five ideas.

Open season is now declared on the master list. The time has arrived for open discussion and airing of individual views on the matter. The object of this exercise is to boil the list of twenty-five ideas down to the five best ideas which have been suggested by the subteams. Naturally, a few of the ideas on the master list will be

Shared Participation

eliminated through duplication of thought. The rest must be hammered out patiently in group discussion, as the combined knowledge and experience of the entire group is brought to bear on testing each idea and judging the worth of all to select the five best ideas the group has to offer.

Wider evaluation comes next. The five-man subteams re-form into their original groups of ten men each to consider a total of ten ideas (five from each subteam). By now, all aspects of the problem should be clearly understood by all the participants, and it is the task of each ten-man team to analyze all the proposed ideas for solutions until, by group decision, the ten ideas are reduced once more to the five which the ten-man team has finally judged to be the most important and useful ideas.

At this point, the individual voices of the team figuratively become one voice. Each team has arrived at a consensus—five ideas or solutions which meet with the approval of every member of the team. And each ten-man team chooses one of its number to represent the team in presenting its five ideas or solutions to management. Since this representative speaks for a group, total honesty is expected and valued. This completes the third stage of the Shared Participation process, the step we call Consensus.

The fourth and final step is called Commitment. This step consists of a meeting between a management panel and members of the participating teams. Although all team members may attend, only the chosen representatives of each team actually confer with the management panel. Any other form of discussion would tend to become unwieldy.

Ideally, the management panel should include approximately half a dozen persons. Possible participants might be the company's purchasing agent, the chief engineer, the plant manager, the sales manager, or any other administrative representatives. The important thing is that the management team should be able to respond objectively and constructively to the ideas and solution offered by the consulting teams. It would obviously also make sense to involve those management officials whose areas of concern are touched by the problem being taken under consideration.

During this interlevel discussion of the pros and cons of each of the final ideas submitted, the management panel may even see fit to introduce additional information of which the employees on the participating teams were previously unaware. In this event, it may become necessary for the consulting teams to regroup and review this new material, in order to modify or augment their previous recommendations to management.

Free discussion between the employees' teams and the management panel continues until everybody can agree on the solutions and ideas to be implemented. What follows is a commitment that by the nature of formulation transcends ordinary management-labor agreements.

Through the Shared Participation process, this commitment has been made by employee to employee, management to employee, employee to management, and management to management. Everybody's best ideas have been drawn together to form a strong, binding knot. All parties are equally committed to act on the recommendations which have been mutually approved, and at this point, a time schedule is established for the implementation of each idea or solution, with shared responsibility to follow through assigned to both management and employee representatives.

Follow-Through—the final step in Shared Participation—culminates in a review meeting, three or four weeks after the final Commitment meeting. The purpose of the review meeting is to examine results of the program and to determine that all of the ideas and solutions agreed upon have indeed been implemented. It may even be necessary to hold a second or a third review meeting in order to make absolutely sure that all goals have been met, or changed with the additional knowledge and experience.

The special power of Shared Participation stems from the fact that it stretches across the board and effectively breaks down traditional communication barriers. It provides management with unlimited access to valuable information from sublevels of the organization; and it can also do much to reverse or at least ameliorate workers' and management's traditionally jaded views. The psychological benefits of mutual understanding through mutual effort cannot be underestimated. But even more important, Shared Participation pays its way in pragmatic terms.

Properly formulated and applied, Shared Participation

decisions have generally proved to be more effective than most individual decisions. It's plain common sense—they have to be. If you put twenty or thirty people's combined knowledge and experience and intuition in a pot, you have just got to come up with a better decision or solution than you could possibly obtain from a single individual, no matter how knowledgeable or experienced that individual might be. The Shared Participation plan is simple, it's concise, it's easily workable, it's practical and it's economical. Its only natural enemy is the Old Authoritarian Way—the tired standby of tired management. Oh, maybe they get a say in where the company picnic will be held this year, but employees should be pulled in on decisions which could affect their efficiency and ultimately produce a better product or service.

Obviously, the concept of Shared Participation will not strike everybody as the best idea they've ever heard. To those business executives who rely heavily on authoritarian traditions, Shared Participation may appear to loom as a threat to their managerial prerogatives. They may even suspect it smells slightly of revolution. But they could not be more mistaken.

We do not envision Shared Participation as a replacement for authoritarian decision-making. Rather, we view it as an alternative—a supplementary method of widening the range of involvement and commitment in order to build dynamic organizations. The benefits to management in terms of improved employee understanding of the company's problems are inestimable and could even be felt eventually at the bargaining table.

Shared Participation

Consider the hard-headed, veteran blue-collar worker, who hides a wealth of useful ideas and imagination under a crusty, complaining, anti-management façade. For years, he's been muttering to himself about the vast improvements, the enormous beneficial changes that would take place practically overnight if he were running the show. It's a favorite lunchtime topic of conversation among workers, and it usually begins with the words, "If I were the boss . . ." All right. Now instead of talking about it, he's got a chance to help find a solution to a given problem. He's got a chance to put his money—in this case, his knowledge and experience—where his mouth is.

As a member of the five-man subteam, the employee pulls his thoughts together and puts his five best ideas down on paper. Privately, he's convinced that they are the five best ideas in the world on that particular subject. When his ideas are tossed into the hopper with the others and further lists are compiled, our would-be world-beater may suffer a pang of disappointment when he notices that other members of both his team and the other team have also thought of a couple of the ideas he thought were so original. That's bad enough for his ego. But what really throws him is that there on the list are a couple of other ideas—ideas that hadn't even occurred to him—which he has to admit are even better than his own. Already, he's feeling the effects of added inputs of knowledge and experience which can't help but benefit his company in the long run. First, he has learned something; and secondly, he has less to mutter about.

Shared Participation 73

Remember that old adage about how you can't make a silk purse out of a sow's ear? When you're starting out with Shared Participation, you can't expect a chronic mutterer to put in a prize-winning performance as a decision-maker the first time out without any coaching. At least in its initial stages, Shared Participation is going to require a little pre-training and help for those participants who are not accustomed to making decisions. Realistically, we must face the fact that a worker whose opinions and suggestions are being sincerely solicited for the first time (and he may have been with the company for many years) may not be totally prepared for the honor. He may very possibly react emotionally or dogmatically to a problem, and this attitude, although understandable, could cancel out the potential benefits of his invaluable knowledge, experience and intuition.

At ABS, we have introduced an exercise developed by NASA to demonstrate the intricacies of decision by consensus. The exercise is called The Moon Problem, and it describes the predicament of a space crew scheduled to rendezvous with a mother ship on the lighted surface of the moon. As a result of mechanical difficulties, the ship has been forced to land 200 miles from the point of rendezvous. Both the ship and its contents were damaged in the landing in such a way that only fifteen items of equipment and supplies are left unscathed. The point of the problem is to list these fifteen items in order of their importance in assisting the crew to complete the 200-mile trip to the mother ship in safety. Here is a list of the items, which we ask our team members to number in order of importance. (If you feel like trying the exercise yourself before reading on, you'll find the key at the end of the chapter.)

1. Box of matches
2. Food concentrate
3. Fifty feet of nylon rope
4. Parachute silk
5. Portable heating unit
6. Two .45-caliber pistols
7. One case dehydrated Pet Milk
8. Two 100-pound tanks of oxygen
9. Stellar map (of the moon's constellation)
10. Life raft
11. Magnetic compass
12. Five gallons of water
13. Signal flares
14. First-aid kit, containing injection needles
15. Solar-powered FM receiver-transmitter

The key to this exercise was also prepared at NASA, where the pooled knowledge and experience of moon travel and exploration makes solution of this problem a relatively easy one. At ABS, it serves as an excellent illustration of how pooled knowledge and experience can improve the general knowledge and experience of a five- or ten-man team, and as a result, improve its chances of coming up with a "right" answer.

If you have tried the moon problem yourself, you'll have discovered by now that it's not as simple as it looks, and it's easy to understand why its solution has led to a

Shared Participation 75

great deal of argument and discussion among groups at ABS. At one session, a Cleveland police captain—a man whose general knowledge was impressive and whose views on most subjects were extremely sound—became stubborn on one point: he insisted that one of the space crew's primary needs would be the magnetic compass, and he kept on insisting on this point until another team member quietly reminded him that the compass would be totally useless on the surface of the moon, which has no magnetic field. A number of others, wrestling with the problem, have clung to the box of matches as a vital item. They're probably former boy scouts, but they are forgetting the fact that without oxygen, the matches will not ignite and are therefore quite useless.

But the moon problem serves to point out another fact. The judgment of any group is only as good as the knowledge, experience and creativity of its participants. Since we have few moon explorers or NASA-trained scientists in our labs, any group consensus on this problem will definitely be flawed. It is essential that the problem to be solved be one in which the majority of the group has knowledge and experience. Not every ranking of items in order of importance will meet with everyone's complete approval, but that doesn't matter. Unanimity is no more of a goal than majority agreement. It is not necessary for every team member to be as satisfied with every ranking as he would be, for instance, if he had complete control of the group. What is important is that he be able to accept a ranking on the grounds of logic and that he can accept a judgment as feasible. All group members must arrive at this point of minimal agreement before the decision can rightly be called a group decision, or a decision by consensus. To help our teams at ABS to avoid the obvious pitfalls, we offer a list of do's and don'ts to bear in mind while striving for consensus:

1. Avoid arguing for your own rankings. Present your position as lucidly and as logically as you can. But pay attention to the reactions of the group, and take these into consideration before pressing any point of your argument.

2. Avoid "win-lose" stalemates in discussing rankings. Discard the notion that differences of opinion mean that someone must win and someone must lose. When an impasse occurs, look for the next most acceptable alternative for both sides.

3. Avoid changing your mind only in order to avoid conflict. Don't sacrifice your views for the sake of agreement and harmony. Withstand pressures to yield which have no objective, logically sound foundation. Strive for enlightened flexibility. Avoid outright capitulation.

4. Avoid conflict-reducing techniques such as the majority vote, averaging, bargaining, coin-flipping, and the like. These are cop-outs. Treat differences of opinion as indicative of an incomplete sharing of relevant information. Press for additional information-sharing when it seems necessary and in order.

5. View differences of opinion as natural and helpful, rather than as hindrances to decision-making. Generally speaking, more ideas mean more conflict; but they also mean a richer array of resources for the whole group.

6. View initial agreement as suspect. Explore the reasons underlying apparent agreements. Make sure that

those in agreement have arrived at similar solutions for the same basic reasons or for complementary reasons before allowing such solutions to be incorporated into the group decision.

If these rules are respected and followed with care, they can serve as guidelines to the least experienced decision-maker and bring his additional knowledge and experience into play as part of a Shared Participation team. It's simply a question of familiarizing a person with techniques that at present lie beyond his grasp.

There is no reason why the Shared Participation process cannot be applied to a whole host of problems which are today usually resolved by groping, stumbling, trial, and many errors. Take the relations between men and women. Why could they not work out their age-old misunderstandings in the same way that members of an organization or corporation do?

Suppose a group of five men and five women were given a specific problem concerning the relations between male and female. The participants would write down their ideas and the suggestions pooled in the way we've discussed. These suggestions would then be kicked around until a consensus was reached. I believe the process would not only prove rewarding, but surprising as well, because no one would know which suggestions had been made by males and which by females. The submerging of such sexual bias, which is always the cause of hot contention and even hostility, would undoubtedly pay handsome dividends in bringing the sexes closer. The aggravating and inaccurate phrase "just like a man" or "just like a woman" might even disappear from common speech.

The ultimate survival of our society depends on our making dramatic changes in our present management systems. In the business world of today, employees and unions routinely make exorbitant demands. Management, just as routinely, locks the workers out of the vital processes of policy-setting and decision-making, without concern for what these attitudes mean in terms of the welfare of the company or the worker. To survive, we must learn to work together in a spirit of equal trust and true cooperation.

A manufacturer friend of mine told me a story which illustrates the mutual disadvantages of the present system. At his plant, a machine on the production line began doing something wrong, with the result that an intricate part in a small mechanical device the company manufactured was being inserted several millimeters out of place, leaving no space for the other parts. A foreman, and finally the superintendent of production examined the misperforming machine for a full hour, with no success. Baffled, they called on the vice-president in charge of production, who inspected the machine and couldn't put his finger on the problem either. After a while, the machine operator (who'd stepped back in order to allow his superiors to tackle the problem) mumbled a simple suggestion which turned out to be a practical one, correcting the machine's misfunction and putting the production line back in motion. When it was all over, the vice-president turned to the worker and vented his exasperation. "Why the hell didn't you say that

Shared Participation 79

an hour ago?" he thundered. The worker shouted back defiantly, "Because you never asked me!" It was true. Nobody had thought to solicit a suggestion from the man closest to the machine. It was a clear case of "Here, let me handle this"—without a backward thought for the man's experience and knowledge—or his feelings.

We foresee that by 1980, employees and unions will share responsibility for the survival and growth of their companies with management. Hopefully, the welfare of all will have superseded the selfish points of view that persist today on both sides.

A fantastic dream? I don't think so. I like to think of myself as an idealistic realist. It would be unrealistic to predict that all management decisions will be made by the Shared Participation method by the year 1980. But I do believe it is fair to predict that intelligent, enlightened management will use this system for decision by consensus whenever feasible.

If these responsibility-sharing techniques are adopted in even 80 per cent of all management decisions, not only will the quality of those decisions be considerably improved, but also, the corporate chief won't be faulted for the relatively small percentage of decisions which for reasons of immediacy, he must make alone in the Old Authoritarian Way.

(Key to the moon problem: 15, 4, 6, 8, 13, 11, 12, 1, 3, 9, 14, 2, 10, 7, 5.)

V. Charting a Course Through Life

One Labor Day weekend, the United States Coast Guard picked up two teen-aged boys drifting off the shore of a bustling New England resort town in a stolen motorboat. Later, the boys admitted to the police that they had stolen the boat in order to travel to Florida, where they'd heard they could earn a lot of money working as bellhops for the winter tourist season. How had they planned to reach their destination? Well, they had a map—a road map of the United States published by a well-known oil company.

It's easy to laugh at the youngsters' nautical naïveté. Everybody knows you can't pilot a boat from New England to Florida with the help of nothing but a road map. What you need to make the voyage safely are nautical charts—sailors' maps to show you where the shoals lie hidden and where the rocks that can tear your craft apart are concealed by full tides.

Sure, everybody knows that. And yet most of us plow through life with the equivalent of a road map to steer us through the stormy seas and chancy channels of human existence. Buffeted and confused, we never think to ask for better directions. Sometimes, like the young boatnapers, we cut our engines and drift because we fear hidden dangers, and drawbacks of which we are only dimly aware. We consider ourselves fortunate if we manage to stay afloat.

"Don't rock the boat" is an all-too-familiar cry, which human beings utter whenever they feel threatened. We reject the risks of moving ahead in the darkness of our self-ignorance. If we don't drown, that's good enough, isn't it? Who cares if we don't move ahead? Yet if we had better directions, if we were armed with the right charts, we could skirt many of the hazards—both real and imagined—and we could get much further ahead in life, at a much faster clip.

The object of the behavioral science laboratory is to provide people with better directions for making their way through life. Anybody who experiences a laboratory session at ABS leaves that adventure armed with the equivalent of a personalized nautical chart—or if you prefer, a better "road map" of his life. He has been made aware of behavioral patterns and attitudes that may have been seriously impeding his progress in his career or in his personal life. He learns to listen to other people and to receive valuable navigational signals from their behavior toward him. And if he so desires, he can use this new knowledge—he can scan the markings on his chart and employ his new ability to listen—in order to avoid familiar pitfalls and to improve his over-all performance in life. He has a much clearer picture of where he is going and why, as well as much more detailed directions on how to reach his destination. Some remarkable examples of the benefits provided by these new maps and markings have emerged from our work at ABS.

Harry C. was a reporter on a metropolitan daily newspaper, a career goal he'd set his heart on as a small boy. When he came to ABS, he was pushing forty-five, and a kind of bitterness was starting to creep into his attitude toward his work. He was just beginning to realize that he was not achieving the degree of success he had hoped for as a youth. He saw that so far, he had fallen far short of what he considered to be his potential. What Harry had to face was the fact that he had ripened into a run-of-the-mill reporter, consistently assigned to run-of-the-mill stories. Dairy-show openings, ribbon-cutting ceremonies, Chamber of Commerce luncheons: Harry covered them all. And while he was making his humdrum rounds, the bright newcomers ("the college kids," as Harry called them) got the juicy, front-page, byline assignments and the investigative feature stories that win journalistic prizes.

Charting a Course Through Life 83

Harry was very well aware of what had happened to him in his career, but he didn't have the faintest idea of why it had happened. Like many another disappointed person, Harry blamed his lack of progress squarely on everybody else—a managing editor who didn't like him, a city editor who bore him some kind of grudge. The details of these fanciful vendettas were understandably hazy, and the only person besides Harry who believed his excuses was Harry's wife, who accepted them out of loyalty to her husband.

A week in a laboratory session at ABS not only pointed out to Harry the extent of his self-delusion, it cured him of it. As the week wore on, he realized that the real fault for the stagnant state of his career was his own behavior. His laboratory mates showed him how he really appeared to both his co-workers and his superiors at the newspaper.

Harry's biggest problem was that he took great pride in his store of general knowledge, and this pride led him to proceed almost entirely on assumptions. He never bothered looking anything up—he was fond of bragging that he didn't have to. Harry was always one step ahead of everybody else—or so he imagined—with "the real dope." What's more, he stubbornly insisted that his information was The Word and would brook no discussion on the subject. Harry's preconceived ideas on everything from art to the war in Vietnam made it virtually impossible for him to achieve the state of objectivity and receptiveness vital to good news reporting. His editors couldn't trust Harry with a big news story because they knew there was always the danger that he wouldn't be able to see beyond his nose to the true facts of the story, that he might hamper his reporting efforts by relying on his preconceptions. So instead, they sent him trotting off to ribbon-cutting ceremonies, where he'd have nothing more to bring back than the name of the big shot who cut the ribbon.

At ABS, Harry learned to listen to others—something he hadn't done since he was a cub reporter. He learned to listen at ABS because the others in the group forced him to listen. When he started off on a know-it-all tack, the group shut him up; and by the end of the week, Harry was offering his opinions only when somebody asked for them. Now, it would be unrealistic for us to claim that Harry went back to his old job a new man and became the paper's star overnight. When he walked away from that ABS session, Harry was the same middle-aged man with the same old tendencies to pontificate. But he had been given a marker which enabled him to spot a pontification on the horizon, so when he felt one coming on, if he felt like it, he could shut up in time to save the situation.

It took a while for Harry's modified behavior to attract much notice back in his city room. After all, for years he'd been tagged as a loudmouth and a know-it-all, and old opinions die hard. But after a time, the editors took note of the fact that Harry wasn't coming on as strong as usual. A few months after leaving the laboratory, he sent me a copy of a front-page, byline story—the first such assignment he'd been handed in almost a decade!

In any course of self-improvement, there's a tendency to concentrate one's attentions on anti-social or antagonistic behavior because (1) it's a common fault, which many of us fail to notice in ourselves; and (2) it's conspicuous and therefore easier to tackle. You notice somebody who snarls rudely at other people or sneers at anybody else's suggestions or argues continually about nothing.

What sometimes goes practically unnoticed is the person who does nothing. He doesn't argue, but he doesn't contribute anything, either. This kind of non-behavior or passive non-action can be just as harmful to a person as actively antagonistic behavior. It can prevent a person from enjoying the fullest possible human relationships, and it can hamper a person's progress in the business world. In terms of a chart, this can't be considered a rock or a reef—it's more like a blank spot or a hole. At one of our ABS sessions, the laboratory action showed a businessman there was just such a hole in his life chart and provoked him into doing something about it.

George D. was the president of a small plastics company which was always hovering on the brink of profit. In other words, it never made a very large profit, and the delicate margin between profit and loss had been narrowing of late. George was depressed by this course of events and his depression was compounded by the fact that he felt completely isolated from the rest of the company's employees, including his own executive staff.

What showed up on George's "chart" was something like a reef that lay between him and his employees. The fact was, he had never taken the slightest interest in his employees on any other level than that of sheer productivity. All he knew about his people was what they looked like and what their jobs were. He was interested in production figures and cost sheets, but not in human beings. He only knew the names of a handful of employees, although his firm employed 250 men and women. As long as nobody made any waves, George was content. He took things for granted, accepted a placid façade as a sign of satisfaction, and didn't go looking for trouble.

As a result of George's detached attitude, none of his 250 employees were tempted to confide in him—about themselves or the company's operation, even though they were in a position to see things George couldn't. They knew perfectly well that George didn't like waves, so they very obligingly didn't make any. Then George enrolled in an ABS session, at the urging of a lawyer friend of his who'd just completed the experience.

The workings of the lab session demonstrated to George that he had a firm tendency to sail along on the surface, taking things as they came. He was not in the habit of asking questions; and as a result, he received very few answers. Nobody feels compelled to answer questions before somebody asks them. And in George's case, what he didn't know was hurting—the company. Profits were slipping, and George never asked himself or anybody else, "Why?" The answers to the slipping profits were locked in the heads of the workers he never spoke to.

The laboratory group showed George how to listen and learn by questioning anything he didn't understand. He came to realize that if you want information, you've got to go get it. He went back to his plant determined to cross the reef that lay between him and his workers. The latter were at first astonished by the change in their boss's attitude. He abandoned his ivy tower and plunged into the production department and other areas of the company's operation, asking streams of questions as he moved from one section to another. As he made his inquiries, his employees responded by giving George the answers he required, and little by little, George was able to pull things together and get his company back into the black. The new person-to-person contact was also a warm human experience for George, and it cheered his workers to think that he now regarded them as people, rather than as automatons.

The laboratory session provided George with a chart of his behavioral pattern, including the reef that separated him from his personnel. When he first returned to his company, he went on a real communications binge. Then he began to revert to his old behavior, he began to creep back into his shell and shut himself off once more. Luckily, his new awareness of this behavioral pattern prevented him from reverting completely. As soon as he felt himself starting to withdraw into his old, silent isolation, he caught himself in the act and pushed himself into action, popping into the next office to consult with his vice-president, or paying a visit to the production department to chat with the foreman.

You can teach an old dog new tricks, but that doesn't mean he is going to do them all the time, or even remember them all a week later. Old habits are not only hard to break, sometimes they're unbreakable. But if you're taught to recognize an old, bad habit and be aware of the effect it has on other people, you can at least modify your tendencies in that direction.

If you sail in and out of a certain harbor all your life,

88   Shared Participation

you develop a certain skill in navigating those particular waters. You learn where the trouble spots are, but you still look for the familiar markers—the flasher on the jetty, the red nun buoy off the port bow—every time you sail in or out of that harbor. It's exactly the same with behavioral trouble spots. The laboratory experience provides you with maps and markers. It doesn't erase a behavioral pattern any more than a nautical chart-maker can remove a shoal. All it does is to show you that the behavioral pattern is there, and this knowledge enables you to chart your course around your behavioral problem, to avoid your trouble spot or shoal and move ahead apace.

From the examples I've cited thus far, you might be getting the impression that our sessions at ABS are reserved for businessmen and other community and organizational "leaders," but this is far from being the case. A great many of the people who have come to ABS are ordinary people from ordinary walks of life who come for the same reasons the "leaders" do—to improve their understanding of their own behavior and to apply this knowledge the best they can to improve the quality of their lives.

Not too surprisingly in this day of the liberated woman, we get an impressive number of intelligent young housewives who are seeking more meaningful ways in which to find fulfillment for themselves and their families. One such person, a young wife and mother named Mary Q., carried an air of gloom around like an umbrella.

During the initial stages of her laboratory experience, it became clear that Mary could be counted on to look on the bad side of just about anything. She was the kind of person who when greeted with the remark, "Isn't it a lovely day!" would reply, "Yes, but it's supposed to rain this afternoon." In the course of the free-form discussions, nobody was very much surprised to learn that Mary was unhappy in the role of a housewife and that she felt deeply resentful of her husband, who she felt neglected her. Actually, he didn't neglect her at all, he just left her alone in the house while he went off to work.

Before coming to ABS, Mary had attempted to find her own solutions to her problems. To assuage her feelings of disappointment, she decided to pursue a doctorate in social science. She threw herself into her studies with a vengeance and spent every moment of her spare time poring over her textbooks, which of course did nothing to improve her already unsatisfactory domestic situation.

The laboratory group helped Mary to see that her marriage was foundering on the not-so-hidden rocks of her own persistent pessimism. Mary was aware of her attitude, but she didn't consider it pessimistic. Her term for it was "being realistic." This was her way of making her antisocial behavior more acceptable to herself. But the group finally succeeded in making Mary understand that whatever she wanted to call it, it was downright depressing, day in and day out, and it was probably the very thing that was turning her husband off so effectively to the detriment of her marriage.

Would you believe that Mary turned into a cheerful person and never uttered another discouraging word? Then you'd probably believe that pigs can fly or the Brooklyn Bridge is still for sale. Such a complete transformation would have required a major miracle, and so far, we have only gotten as far as the minor variety. We specialize in the kind of miracle for which a reasonable explanation can easily be found.

All that actually happened in Mary Q.'s case was that the laboratory group showed her that her pessimistic-realistic observations were wrecking her marriage. The rest was up to Mary. When she returned home to her husband, she could use this new information about herself to check her behavior or modify it, so that her husband occasionally heard something else besides end-of-the-world gloom. This course of action couldn't fail to bring about some degree of improvement in the relationship between Mary and her husband. If, on the other hand, Mary chose to tuck her new-found knowledge away in a drawer and save it for "Sunday-best" behavior, the couple's relationship would inevitably continue to deteriorate.

Most people who come to ABS have no more serious problems than anybody else. That is to say, they are moderately satisfied with their lives, and they count their dissatisfactions and disappointments as normal. ABS, after all, is not a psychiatric clinic, nor are we prepared to deal with people who are suffering from serious neuroses or other mental maladjustments. What we can do is to make people more aware of themselves. We open doors of understanding so that instead of "getting along all right," a person can improve his performance and get the very most he can out of life. We're not psychiatrists, and we don't attempt to wrestle with serious psychiatric problems. But once in a while, somebody comes along

Charting a Course Through Life

with a real whopper of a practical problem, and often, the laboratory session can help to solve it.

A forty-year-old New Yorker, Philip P., had already signed up for a laboratory session some weeks before a real crisis developed in his life. In mid-career—you might even have said at the height of his career—he was fired from his job as vice-president and assistant director of a service organization. Philip decided to attend the ABS session anyway, because he believed that it might help him to sort out his ideas about the future. If one were to return to our previous image of a road map, you could best describe the discoveries Philip made during that week by saying that he found out a bridge was down on his road to success.

Philip's missing bridge was the ability to fight for what he believed to be right, for he hated arguments and would go to any extreme to avoid having one with anybody. As a result of this evasive attitude, Philip, in his previous employment, had formed the habit of going along with his boss's decisions on everything, even though he knew perfectly well that in many cases, the boss's judgment was dead wrong and based on inadequate information. Stuck in a web of half-baked decision-making (largely due to his own behavior), Philip suffered from a growing feeling of frustration in his work.

To compensate for this, Philip complained long and loudly behind his boss's back—to his wife, to his friends, finally to anybody who would listen to him when he stopped in at a favorite bar for drinks after work. He began drinking more and enjoying it less. His performance at the office fell off considerably, diminishing to a robotlike round of duties, and the inevitable happened —he got his walking papers.

Once he had managed to digest the bad news and recover partially from his initial shock, Philip was ready with an explanation for his wife and friends. He blamed his firing on his boss because, as he explained, "He knows I'm smarter and I know more about the outfit than he does—that's why he had to get rid of me!" The fact was, Philip's boss didn't know any such thing. He had no way of knowing. Philip had never disagreed with him, volunteered any strong opinions, or pressed any particular point of view, so the vast fund of superior knowledge which Philip boasted of having (and most likely, did have) never came to light.

During his week-long laboratory session at ABS, Philip learned the value of constructive argument and gradually came to realize that by avoiding fights all those years, he had also failed to contribute the most he could to his organization. He had used only a fraction of his intellectual abilities while doing his job. He had given his boss lip service and nothing more—unless you want to count the surface harmony which his non-argumentative habits produced.

In terms of his future prospects, it was a happy coincidence that Philip happened to attend a behavioral science laboratory at this crucial point in his career. The lab helped to provide him with a map of his behavior which he could then use to get himself back on the road to success—this time, ready to contribute fully to the growth of his company—and himself.

Sometimes, these charts that evolve from laboratory

sessions do more than just show one person a clear view of his own life's course. They can also serve as guides to the personalities of others, enabling one to spot qualities and attitudes in other people that may lie hidden below the surface, like the most massive parts of icebergs. The big, gruff policeman turns out to be a tenderhearted reader of poetry; the wisecracking salesman is riddled with self-doubts behind his shell of wisecracks; the shy, mousy housewife is really a tower of strength and a fund of enormous wisdom that she is afraid to express. Contradictions such as these abound in real life, and as we discover these facts about others, are we not helping to discover ourselves?

The foundering that takes place when we don't have all the little roads of life laid out for us is what builds the action into the laboratory experience. As the group gropes through hours of conversational give-and-take toward a plane of mutual understanding and trust, all kinds of paths are plotted, all kinds of channels marked, and all kinds of itineraries mapped out.

Scanning one's personal life map with the aid of the laboratory group's revealing objectivity, one is enabled to spot a wrong turn taken or perhaps even a dead-end road. This valuable information can help a person to avoid wrong turns in the future; it can also prompt him to make a behavioral U-turn in order to make his way out of a non-productive, personal cul-de-sac.

Sometimes, the laboratory experience can provide a participant with just the impetus he needs to dramatically change his life for the better. This was the case of an advertising man, Jim B., who arrived at an ABS session sporting all the outward signs of satisfaction and success. At first meeting, it was easy to categorize Jim as a man of above-average achievement who was getting the most out of life—a person who derived great satisfaction from what he was doing, and did it well.

It developed that there was no question about the latter point. Jim did his job well, all right. In fact, he was a phenomenal success in the world of advertising, where his creative imagination and energetic drive had gotten him almost to the top of the pile. But as the session wore on, it became equally apparent to Jim and to everybody else in the group that his glow of well-being was as much a product of his imagination as his most inspiring advertising campaign. Underneath it all, Jim was not really at all happy in advertising. He really disliked the whole business, but he had managed to bury his personal dissatisfaction by convincing himself that the material status symbols his success had earned for himself and his family were worth the battle and the psychological dissatisfactions.

As the week progressed, Jim became more and more aware of the fact that his boyhood dream of being a teacher was still very much alive. The more he thought about it, the more he realized the core of his discontent. Advertising had failed to give him the rewards he needed in terms of personal satisfaction because basically, for him it was an unfulfilling way to make a living. His strong inclination lay in the field of service. The idea of helping appealed to him greatly, and he badly needed to feel that he was making his most valuable contribution to society. Another man may feel advertising fulfills his needs. The laboratory experience provided Jim with a map that showed him stuck at the end of a dead-end road—a very comfortable dead-end road, to be sure, but a dead-end all the same. It was clear to him that no matter what further material rewards he reaped in the advertising field (and there really wasn't much higher he could go), he was never going to derive complete personal fulfillment in that line of work.

Several months following his session at ABS, Jim made a dramatic change in his career and his life style. He left the advertising agency and the city in which it was located and moved with his family to a small academic community in New Hampshire, where he started a second career in the teaching profession at the age of forty-two. The move cost Jim and his family a good deal in cash and comforts (at least the excessive kind), but the new life style proved to have its own benefits. Jim's wife, who had come from a small town originally, was much happier in the academic community than she had ever been in the city. Also, she found the low-key social life far pleasanter and easier to enjoy than the frantic business of being a "business wife." As far as the children were concerned, the move was also a lucky one. In his new post, Jim had far more time to spend with his sons—time for camping trips and fishing, pastimes he'd been too busy to pursue while enmeshed in his advertising career. The whole family became a closer, warmer unit in the new circumstances of their life.

The path of life is full of pitfalls for the unwary journeyer. Preconceived notions and prejudicial attitudes can hamper a person's total performance enormously, and they're hard to spot without a chart of your behavior. A police chief told me of a discovery he made while attending a laboratory session at ABS.

Another member of the chief's particular group had "hippie" written all over him. He wore beads and blue jeans and shoulder-length hair—the works. The laboratory threw the policeman and the longhair together in a way that would hardly have occurred outside. For a whole week, they were compelled to accept each other on equal terms, and this enabled the policeman to get past the visual image projected by the hippie—to get to know him as a person. "He was very learned and well-educated, a nomad type," the chief recalled later. "He had roamed all over this country and Europe. In talking to him, I found out he was extremely sensitive about his appearance. He was very proud of his beads and the rest of his paraphernalia. Now, after having had this experience, I wouldn't think of making remarks about a person's hair or dress while I was trying to talk to him."

To the chief, who didn't fancy beads or a page-boy bob, his previous attitude toward "hippies"—usually one of mild amusement—had seemed harmless enough. It wasn't until he actually had a chance to converse as an equal with a person wearing beads and a bob that he realized how this apparently innocent attitude could prejudice the other person against him and put a real dent in their ability to communicate with each other.

The further one wishes to explore his potential, the more signposts and charts he can use. When a sailor takes his boat into an unfamiliar harbor or unknown waters, he proceeds more carefully and slowly than he

Charting a Course Through Life

does in his home waters. He keeps one eye on his charts and the other on his destination, moving deliberately and little by little, to avoid an accident.

That's the way it is with life. Whenever we feel like stepping out of a rut or expanding our horizons, we instinctively become cautious and slow down. The laboratory experience gives one maps and markings that make this unnecessary, that show where the rocks and shoals are, so that you can move ahead briskly and with confidence toward any goal.

VI. We Can All Be Heroes

"You can't fight city hall" is an antihero axiom that has seen better days. As a matter of fact, it has just about had it as a truism or a popular attitude. People are getting smarter. The communications explosion has given the average man of today access to far more information than his great-grandfather—or even his father—had. All over the country, individual citizens are tilting at windmills and knocking them down—having a go at "city hall" and coming out on top!

Just take a look at a couple of dramatic examples from

We Can All Be Heroes

the past decade: Eugene McCarthy stood up and said his piece, and Lyndon Johnson retired to his ranch in Texas; Ralph Nader made a fuss about automobile safety, and his name became a generic term for organized consumer protest.

You don't have to agree with the actions or motivations of either of these men to admit that each has made a noticeable change in our society and our way of looking at things—and he accomplished this feat all by himself. That's what heroes are made of—the courage and determination to move ahead and act without the comfort of cohorts. Heroes respond directly to their consciences and perform their feats because they have to.

It is true that heroes are made, not born. Every society produces its own kinds of heroes to take care of its special needs. If we look closely, we can count among ourselves as many heroes as could the Greeks in better days.

A courageous young New York policeman, Frank Serpico, persisted in his efforts to root out corruption within the ranks of the New York City Police Department and was ignored by officials and shot in the head by an unknown assailant for his pains. While recovering in the hospital, Serpico received poison pen letters from anonymous former police buddies, wishing him a speedy nonrecovery and worse. But Serpico stuck to his ideals and continued his crusade undaunted, with the result that the Knapp Commission investigated his and other charges and discovered that, by George, there was a high degree of corruption at all levels of New York's police operation. So today, Serpico's considered a hero, but as he could tell you, becoming a hero takes a lot of stubborn persistence, and the process can be a painful one.

Our herd instinct persists, and individually, we are reluctant to seek the hero's role. "I don't want to be a hero!" is a common cry of the self-concerned. We hesitate to get involved, and we are anxious not to make ourselves at all conspicuous to our neighbors. In an extreme example of this collective cowardice which was widely publicized a few years ago, thirty-eight apartment dwellers watched a young woman being stabbed to death on a New York City street, and not one of them even had the guts to call the police!

This malady is not confined to those of us in the older, supposedly more conservative generation. Even the long-haired young who are held in disdain by many because of their unwillingness to conform to standard, established patterns of social behavior, are themselves horrified by the prospect of being considered "square" by their peers. So their self-assuring acts of non-conformity take on all the attributes of another kind of conformity.

In the big cities, most of our everyday heroes are policemen and firemen. Yet heroes are not found only in these traditional hero-figures. They exist in quiet little cubbyholes of our culture. A small town in Indiana was gently rocked by the quiet actions of a low man on the local municipal totem pole. Dwight G. was a clerk in the town hall. He worked in the department of tax assessment, and he was the only person on deck one morning when a citizen came in to protest the assessment figures on his property.

After examining the citizen's complaint, Dwight G.

We Can All Be Heroes

reacted with characteristic honesty. He agreed with the citizen that the figures were too high and he volunteered the information that in his opinion, the tax assessor had made an error in his calculations. When the matter reached the ears of Dwight's superior, who happened to be that very tax assessor, the official's own reaction was swift and vindictive. First, he denied hotly that he had made a mistake, and secondly, he suspended Dwight from the job he had held for twenty-four years. Then he set about making sure that his "mistake" (which turned out in the end to be a purposeful stroke of minor larceny) would pass unnoticed by his superiors.

Luckily for Dwight G., a local newspaper got wind of the fuss going on at the town hall and printed a story about it. A subsequent bipartisan review of the situation revealed the truth, the tax assessor was fired and indicted, and Dwight G. got his old job back. Routine, perhaps in this day of major violence and nation-rocking scandals—but who can deny that by acting according to his conscience, Dwight G. proved himself to be a hero in the best sense of the word?

Too many of us—including minor officials and clerks like Dwight G.—are all too willing to shirk responsibility when there's the least indication of trouble. We can't be bothered getting involved. It might take time, and it might just backfire. So we avert our eyes, we "don't know anything," we are perfectly happy to "let George do it." We are so wrapped up in avoiding anything that might possibly cause us any personal inconvenience or risk, we ignore the thought of what may happen if George doesn't do it, either. We need many more heroes, and as a society we must reward them—not punish them as we so often do.

A former secretary of mine told me of a scene she'd witnessed while waiting for her bus one morning. For about ten minutes, she watched while scores of pedestrians hurried past and stepped around the prone figure of a shabbily dressed man lying face down by the wall of a large office building. Like the others, my secretary suspected that the man was probably a bum who'd passed out from drinking, but the possibility that the man was really ill nagged at her conscience. She hailed a passing police car and with a patrolman, approached the prone figure. It was lucky she did. There wasn't a trace of alcohol on the man's breath. He had suffered a heart attack. The police sped him to a nearby hospital, and he managed to pull through, thanks to the actions of the only person among dozens of passersby who cared enough to look closer, to find out if he was sick.

You don't have to plunge through hoops of fire to be a hero. In many cases, it's easier than you'd expect to behave heroically. What does it take? Self-awareness and confidence, to begin with; and these just happen to be two of the primary benefits of the laboratory training experience. Sure, the laboratory shows us our faults and our weaknesses; and this knowledge of our defective points is essential to their modification or correction. But at the same time, an equally valuable picture can be taken of our good points, of which we may have been at least as unaware.

We all know people who chronically understate their own abilities and attractions. It's as common a human affliction as the very opposite fault of boasting. Many of us were raised to regard modesty as a much-desired social trait and we demur automatically when anybody suggests we have done particularly well at something. That's false modesty, and it doesn't do anybody a particle of good.

If we are to operate well with all our powers, we must recognize the outermost parameters of these powers. If we constantly denigrate ourselves, we run the danger of coming to believe that we are less effective than we really are. When we underestimate our strengths and our talents, we are damaging our prospects of fulfilling our potentials just as surely as we do when we choose to overlook or ignore faults that are glaring to others. We must be aware of our abilities in order to use them to the fullest extent. We must realize that we are capable of achieving something if we are to have any hope of achieving it. If you look at a 200-pound weight lying on the floor and decide right then and there that you cannot lift it, you never will manage to lift it, because you won't admit you might be able to, and therefore, you'll never try.

Some of the most heartening results we've seen at ABS concern laboratory participants who discover new strengths and abilities and put these tools to work in their everyday life.

After Maurice C., a dynamic political figure from a small northwestern city, attended an ABS session, he was so enthusiastic about the self-discoveries he had made that he talked his wife into attending a week-long lab. That she agreed to do so went without saying, for

Selma C. always did everything her husband asked her to do.

In fact, Selma C. appeared to be the exact opposite of her outgoing, outspoken husband. While he exuded confidence and leadership, Selma was quiet and docile— a born follower. Her habit of deferring to her husband was so deeply ingrained that when she arrived at the ABS session by herself, she immediately transferred this habit of deference to the other members of her laboratory group.

During the general, free-form discussions, Selma contributed little. Her reactions to those who tried to draw her out were zero. Taking part in the decision-by-consensus exercises, she seemed to lean on other people's opinions instead of formulating her own original ideas. She appeared to have no faith at all in her own judgment.

As the week progressed, Selma's strengths began to show through. They became obvious first to the group, then to Selma herself. What became apparent was that Selma had a keen intelligence which had rusted a little from disuse, but was otherwise in good working order. And when pressed, she exhibited a streak of silent determination that withstood any attempts at interference. Once Selma arrived at a decision, after due consideration, she stuck to her guns.

The lessons of the laboratory were put to good use soon after Selma returned home from the session. Driving to the city from her suburban home, she noticed three men with surveying equipment, getting out of a station wagon near a large county park. On her way home, she noticed that another car had joined the station wagon and that a fourth man had joined the surveying team. As she passed the scene, she recognized the fourth man as a real estate developer.

That night, Selma told her husband what she had seen. When he failed to clear up the mystery, Selma took action herself. The following morning, she called the park department to inquire as to why surveyors should be surveying a public parkland. An embarrassed-sounding official tried to fend Selma off with a noncommittal answer, and there was a time when Selma would have let it go at that. But now, armed with her new self-confidence, Selma flatly refused to accept his official explanation. After spending most of the rest of the day on the telephone, Selma discovered that the park department with the full knowledge of a handful of high city officials had agreed to sell an outlying section of the park land to the developer, and that he planned to build one hundred housing units on the property.

Selma's investigation of the matter might have ended there, for she also discovered that through some dishonest wheeling and dealing, the sale had been made legally, so that the developer had every right to claim the property. Again, it's safe to assume that before her laboratory experience, Selma would have shrugged her shoulders at this point and given up the ghost. Instead, she called a number of prominent citizens and informed them about the plans to desecrate the park acreage. Within days, an action committee had been formed, a petition had been drawn up and signed by thousands of like-minded persons, and as a result, the city's agreement with the developer was annulled.

Shared Participation

The environmental field is full of heroes like Selma—people who have become aware of the perils of ignoring conservation and pollution and are matter-of-factly doing their best to put things right. Sometimes, they use unorthodox methods. But there is a better way. An intelligent-thinking society with enlightened corporations oriented toward social responsibility as well as profit can easily eradicate the severe pollution which began before we all were aware of its dangers.

Like the Marines, heroes have a way of coming to the rescue of beleaguered citizens. One such hero was Jack G., a black man who raised the rent strike to respectability as a method of expressing citizen protest.

G. lived in a substandard apartment building where the walls were crumbling, water dripped everywhere, and rats and roaches played hide and seek with the tenants. One day, G. reached the limits of his patience. Like most of the other tenants, he had tried repeatedly to persuade the landlord to do something about his building. Calls went unanswered, and no repairmen ever showed up.

At the end of his tether, G. called a meeting of the tenants in the building and, with their co-operation, called a rent strike against the landlord. The move was a desperate one. There was the chance that G. and his friends would be evicted for non-payment of rent. But as it happened, his drastic action drew attention to the landlord's violations of at least a dozen building code regulations, and in the end, the landlord was compelled by the courts to put his property in order.

At the time when Jack G. tried it, the rent strike

was still kind of touch and go, but his example encouraged others to take similar measures and also established precedents that led to widespread use of the rent strike as a practical protest technique. The rent strike ultimately came to be sanctioned by many city halls across the country, and municipal authorities in many cities will supply protesting tenants with printed instructions on how to organize co-operative strikes in order to gain their lawful rights.

The idea of one man against many is a staple of the *High Noon* school of American drama, including the non-Western variety. A perfect example of the effect of one man's convictions upon a group of his peers was offered in a movie called *Twelve Angry Men,* which involved the deliberations of a jury following a murder trial.

A typically convincing Hollywood hero, Henry Fonda, played the pivotal role in the drama. According to testimony at the trial, a Puerto Rican stood accused of stabbing a man to death in a New York tenement building. The youth's future rested precariously on the damning testimony of a man who lived in an apartment across the way from the tenement, separated by elevated railway tracks. This man claimed to have witnessed the murder. There was also a policeman who testified that the murder weapon, a knife, belonged to the defendant.

At first, the jury's deliberations didn't seem destined to break any records. One juror was in a hurry to get to a ball game. Another was out to punish somebody—he didn't care who—for an injustice he had suffered recently. And still another had it in for Puerto Ricans.

It looked as though the movie was going to end after only about twenty minutes. Then Fonda, calm as ever, threw a monkey wrench into everybody's getaway plans. The policeman who'd identified the murder weapon said there were witnesses who could back up his statement that the knife in question belonged to the defendant. He had stated emphatically that the knife used in the stabbing could be traced without doubt to the Puerto Rican boy.

Now in the jury room, Fonda reached lazily in his pocket and tossed a knife onto the table. The rest of the jurors froze in amazement. The knife was identical to the one shown as Exhibit A. The first shadow of doubt was cast on what seemed like a foolproof case. Obviously, the knife was a common type, and there were probably a thousand of them tucked into a thousand different pockets in New York alone.

Under Fonda's stubborn prodding, the jury reviewed what it had heard and came up with more shadows of doubt. The witness from the tenement across the way had claimed he was awakened by the victim's screams. Yet another witness had established the fact that an elevated train was roaring by at the time of the murder, so how could the first witness have heard the screams?

An elderly, bespectacled juror raised another question, one that had occurred to him previously, but which he had been unwilling to press on his own initiative. The tenement dweller on the witness stand was a woman of about his own age—around sixty-six—and the elderly juror had noticed tiny red marks on either side of her nose, at eye level. Silently, he'd remarked to himself that this was probably a person who habitually wore glasses, but was too vain to wear them during the trial. Now that the other questions had been raised, the elderly juror thought back to his silent observation and voiced his thoughts to the others. He wondered how it was possible for a person who wore glasses all the time—continually enough for them to leave marks on her skin—to see clearly across the approximately 150 feet of space which separated her room from the room in which the murder took place.

In this way, little by little, the jury chewed away at the prosecution's case until, in the minds of all, not a single shred of concrete evidence remained against the defendant. Even the baseball fan was forced to reconsider his initial reactions and opinion. The final verdict was "innocent." And a youth could go free, thanks to the stubborn convictions of a lone holdout—a silent hero who was not afraid or ashamed to swim against the tide.

That's the stuff of which movies are made, even when they're based on real-life incidents. Life is mainly composed of less dramatic encounters, homelier circumstances and less jarring conflicts. But that doesn't mean that we cannot still be heroes—that we cannot make our influence felt in smaller ways. You don't have to make headlines to be considered a hero. A hero is really anybody who sticks his neck out and acts according to his conscience, no matter how much pressure he gets from people who'd rather hang on to the status quo. A hero doesn't buy pat slogans like, "That's the way we've always done it," "Sorry, buddy, but that's the way the system works," or "It's too bad, but there's nothing I can do about it." He marches to the cadence of a different drummer—going it alone, if necessary, to do what he thinks is right. That courageous young policeman Frank Serpico was certainly aware of the risks involved when he blew the whistle on his fellow patrolmen. He knew they all had guns and that at least some of them wouldn't hesitate to use them to protect their reputations and their lucrative shakedown activities. As a matter of fact, he did get shot; but he still went ahead and blew the whistle. He couldn't have lived with himself if he hadn't, and this situation, to a person with a healthy conscience, would be almost as bad as a bullet in the head.

The world is in such bad shape today, the need for heroes has become acute. We can use as many as we can manufacture at every level of our society. The Peace Corps and the Vista volunteer program are good examples of attempts to make the hero role attractive, to interest citizens, particularly the young, in performing useful jobs for practically nothing—their only reward the personal satisfaction that comes from helping one's fellow man. When it was first established, the Peace Corps was swamped with applications from people of all ages and from all walks of life. This proves that our heroic instincts are in relatively good shape and that we are capable of responding nobly when we are properly challenged.

The ABS laboratory experience teaches people to extend themselves, to go beyond their normal limits and outperform themselves. It shows us how to excel in life, how to make the most of every moment and every opportunity. The person who has reached the maximum degree of self-awareness and can recognize his full potential never has to look back with regret on roads not taken. By meeting every challenge, he satisfies himself that he has done and is doing his best.

Our influence on others depends to a large extent on how much we sincerely want to influence others. Of course, there are some people who couldn't care less. They mind their own business and expect others to mind theirs. They don't sign any petitions or knock on any doors—or even, sometimes, vote. They tread water all their lives, leaving the world no better or worse for their having dwelt in it. Even though they pride themselves on "not complaining," they are just as ineffective as those people who are always complaining about something, but never do anything about it.

You may or may not agree with the aims and objectives of the Women's Liberation Movement. Like any revolutionary movement, it has its share of crackpots and radicals. But the backbone of Women's Lib is provided by honestly concerned people who are seeking intelligently to influence social attitudes toward females, and because they care enough, their influence is being felt in every corner of our society—in the arts, in the schools, in consumer affairs, the professions and last, but not least, at the polls.

Who would have believed it possible—say five years ago—that a woman (and a black woman, at that) could capture 5 per cent of the primary vote in Florida, running against a field of seasoned white male pols that included George Wallace, Edmund Muskie, Hubert Humphrey, and George McGovern? Surely, this is a good sign for the future of American females. Already, everyone in the country has been made aware of the goals of Women's

Lib. Some just rail at it, because they feel old values are being threatened. But at its best, the movement represents the chance for a better shake for every woman in the country—including those who cling to their traditional roles.

Our ability to function as influential human beings depends on how much confidence we have and how aware we are of our own behavior and that of the people around us. The person who has trained himself or herself to try to be a better person becomes a more influential person as a result. To do the very best we can—whether in a little pond or a big pond—should be the goal of every wide-awake, decent human being. And it's a goal that the laboratory experience can help one to attain.

As we've mentioned before, we get people from all walks of life and from every level of achievement at our ABS sessions. We deal with giants of industry and commerce—men accustomed to exerting influence—and we help them to see how they can do even better. We do the same with "97-pound weaklings," who for one reason or another, feel that they have no sphere of influence.

A college junior at one of our laboratory sessions astonished his senior companions by launching into a tirade against campus revolutionaries. He came from a university where a tragic bombing incident had taken place, and the event had shocked him profoundly. He'd been haunted ever since by the senselessness of the tragedy.

Never much of a joiner, the student had never gotten involved with the Students for Democratic Action, the John Birch Society, or any other organization—on or off

We Can All Be Heroes 113

campus. His whole attitude was a study in cool detachment. He minded his business, he attended his classes, and he concentrated on his studies. The bombing incident had angered him, but he was still, basically, too much of a devotee of disengagement to do anything about it.

During the week he spent at ABS, the young man became aware of the depth of his detachment and also of the effect it had on others. The other members of the group tried to prod him into committing himself in some way. He seemed not to care about anything or anyone but himself and his academic ambitions. In the group's eyes, the student's precious "non-involvement" came out clearly as selfishness, and they told him so. Challenged by the remarks of his laboratory mates, the student protested. But he had to hustle to convince anybody that he did care, that he did feel strongly about anything—including the violence on his own campus and other campuses across the nation.

As is often the case, nothing earth-shaking followed—if you measure earth tremors only by headlines or seismographic readings. But in a small, subtle way, an influence had been extended, making possible a change for the better. A complacent, rather self-centered young man became less so for knowing more about himself. Through his encounter with the laboratory group, the student learned how to turn his attention outward from himself and to become involved in the world around him. Last heard of, several weeks after his ABS experience, he had decided to run for the student council on a moderate, anti-violence ticket. He may not win the campus election, but as far as we're concerned, he is well on his way to being a winner in much bigger ways. For the first time in his life, he's putting his ideas into action, taking a stand and attempting to influence others to believe that his views are the most reasonable and should, therefore, prevail. It doesn't matter whether or not he wins the campus election. He's done his best, and especially when compared with how he previously performed, that means he's behaving like a hero.

We can all be heroes if we but try. The more we seek to understand, the more we come to know about ourselves and how our behavior affects others, the further we can stretch our imaginations and our intellects to influence others in ways that may presently lie just beyond our ken.

VII. A Company Is Not a Building

Some years ago, a major New England daily newspaper got too big for its building in the center of the city and built and moved to a multi-million-dollar building on the edge of town.

From the outside, the new plant drew an architectural blank. The building was undistinguishable from a bottling plant or a bakery. But inside, the latest thing in four-color presses and other machinery hummed out four-color advertisements and other wonders that, from the publisher's point of view, made the move worthwhile. No expense had been spared to equip the new building with the finest mechanical marvels available. Well, almost.

When the noise and the dust of construction had died down and official scissors had sawed their way through the inevitable ceremonial ribbon, the men in the city room, which was located on the second floor of the building, made a discovery. There was no way for them to get rough copy down to the composing room below, and conversely, there was no way for the composing room to return galleys and clips to the city room.

There was no old-fashioned but reliable pneumatic tube system, as there had been in the old building; and no new-fangled, high-speed apparatus had been substituted. In the general hustle to install high-speed presses and other modern miracles, this small but absolutely vital detail of the newspaper's over-all operation had been completely overlooked. There was no way to get the good news from point A to point B, let alone from Ghent to Aix.

To fill the gap until a suitably modern system could be ordered and installed, a hole was cut in the city room floor, and through this, copy and proofs were passed up and down on "fishing lines" made of kitchen twine. Cynics called it a triumph of human ingenuity over technical progress, but it illustrates a point we should all bear in mind: A company is not a building, and vice versa.

A business plant, however much it cost physically or how modern its equipment and machinery, is still only

A Company Is Not a Building

an inanimate object. What is really of value is the human element, the men who make it run—the brains, the strength and the other human talents housed by the building. It is precisely these human assets that one should consider when evaluating any company or institution—unless you're in the real estate business and are concerned solely with square footage and location.

Perhaps you drive a certain route to work every day, and on the way, you pass a large store or an industrial company. If that's the nearest you ever get to that company, you will naturally tend to think of that company in terms of what it looks like on the outside—a brick façade or concrete walls, a large, blue neon sign, or perhaps outsized, old-fashioned gold letters, spelling out the name of the firm. Large-paned windows, or perhaps no windows at all. Whatever the physical attributes, it is this image of the business organization which enters the consciousness of a casual passerby and stays there. It's all he can be expected to know of the firm.

Many business leaders have displayed a tendency to allow themselves to be beguiled by architecture and decoration. And while polishing up the handles on their big front doors, they've neglected to maintain the same keen degree of interest or pay the same amount of attention to the men who work for them. Their personnel techniques might be nowhere near as modern as the building.

Appearances do count, of course, but it's useless to concentrate everything on what the visitor will see as he comes up the driveway or into the reception hall. He may be impressed, but what probably concerns him most if he's a potential customer or client, is the quality of the work produced at the plant—and that means people.

It is people's brains and imaginations that one should take into account in evaluating any company or institution. They are worth infinitely more to any organization than the building it occupies or the physical equipment and "things" that go on its inventory lists. If a building burns down, it can be rebuilt and equipment can be purchased. The costs are covered by insurance. A building is, therefore, totally replaceable. Not so the people who work in the building. You cannot separate an organization from the people who staff it. Their functions and their productive interrelationships are vital. Take the people out of any organization and what do you have left? A catalogue of items, occupying a certain amount of space in a building—a warehouse shell.

When we say at ABS that we can help business organizations (or for that matter, any kind of organization) we are talking about the people inside those organizations. Because it is the people who have organizational objectives. It is the people who need a division of labor. It is the people who do the work or provide the service. It is the people who need and run meetings, who need and dictate directives, it is the people who need and establish policies. It is the people who need to define methods of delegating tasks. It is the people who need controls. And finally, it is the people who need to learn more about their own behavior so that they will know how to get the most out of themselves and others. Machines can't learn. They have their maximum performances built into them.

A Company Is Not a Building

This may seem like a very obvious thing to say, but believe me, it's a message that seems to pass a lot of people by. There's a blind spot—a defective kind of reasoning that seems to survive almost any degree of laboratory training. It happens all the time, and it continues to amaze us at ABS. Having gone through the intensive laboratory experience, a man will return to his work and his family and ponder what he has learned. Sooner or later, he writes back, "I am a better man. There's no doubt about it. The session really did wonders for me, but I'm not sure how much good it's going to do for my company." Isn't that unbelievable? A company spends fortunes, searching out and hiring the best men it can find, and yet a person who by his own admission has "bettered" himself by seeking to learn more about his own behavior can't understand what good that will do for his company!

As economic considerations have forced industry to move away from the urban centers into suburban areas, management has been forced to take notice of the most basic material needs of its personnel. The old building in the heart of town was surrounded by stores and places to eat. There was probably a favorite sandwich shop across the street or on the corner.

In its new location in a suburban belt, the company is totally isolated from public transportation routes and shopping areas with sandwich shops and restaurants. To make up for the lack of these conveniences, the companies have had to make new provisions for workers, such as parking lots and low-priced but attractive cafeterias with good food and varied menus. This takes care of the workers' physical needs. But at the same time, we have become so entranced with our new buildings—some of which are admittedly very exciting from the architectural point of view—and the zealously landscaped areas surrounding these buildings, that we are running the danger of neglecting the human beings who make things run inside the buildings. We are neglecting them psychologically. We go no further than providing them with a place to park their cars and another place in which to eat. We neglect to strive for greater understanding between management and workers.

We hire gardeners to take care of the lawns, window washers to keep the glass façades gleaming, expensive decorators to transform our lobbies and reception rooms into models of comfort and elegance. But we let the workers go their own way like so many hockey goalies—as long as they don't make mistakes, we don't notice them. And we mistakenly assume that they're okay because they're not setting up any visible barricades or shooting at their executives. This kind of neglect is way out of date, and it can also be expensive.

We all know of incidents between management and workers which have occurred strictly through misunderstanding—incidents which could have been avoided, had those in the positions of influence been more aware of the situation, had they been more aware of the effect of their actions on others. We narrowly averted such an incident at a company we purchased recently.

The company was a three-and-a-half-million-dollar plant, and it was owned by a prominent and successful citizen. He was selling out because the union was grad-

A Company Is Not a Building

ually taking over control of his organization. The union's latest wage demands would have forced the company out of business; and the management could see no hope for negotiating a more equitable settlement with the intransigent union leaders.

We bought the company sixty days before its new contract was due, convinced that despite the fact that the owner of the company was a dynamic, successful individual, there was something he was doing wrong, something of which he himself was unaware. The first thing we did after taking over the company was to conduct a survey of the employees. We asked them to list their five major complaints. Number one turned out to be the parking lot!

Well you might ask, what could be so seriously wrong with a parking lot? If you've seen one parking lot, haven't you seen them all? In the case of the parking facilities here, the employees had two beefs—one perfectly legitimate, the other strictly psychological.

In the first place, the parking lot for employees was an unpaved, unlighted area which could accommodate 450 vehicles. When workers finished work in the evening (or in winter, even in the late afternoon), they often found their cars had been broken into, or dented by others backing out in the blackness. Sometimes, they didn't find their cars at all—they'd been stolen under the cover of darkness. These were solid, legitimate and understandable complaints.

But to add insult to injury, as they made their way into the plant from their own substandard lot, the employees walked right past a paved lot adjacent to the building, where the five top executives parked their company Cadillacs every day. While the executives toiled inside, porters washed the Caddies daily—again, in full view of the work force.

It was understandable, then, that the employees had come to resent the men they worked for. Every day as they walked into the plant in the morning, they looked at those gleaming symbols of affluence parked next to the front door, and thought ill of management. The same emotions were stirred up at lunchtime, and again, at the end of the working day. The workers were venting their wrath in the only way they could think of—by making exorbitant wage demands. The parking lot was the number one obstacle to understanding.

A secondary problem stemmed from the next most important complaint: cold water in the employees' washrooms. The strong prejudices they had already built up against management also led employees to believe that the company's executives were not concerned that no hot water was supplied to the workers. It wasn't a reasonable belief, it was silly—but that's the trouble with not tending your fences and keeping a close watch on morale. People get resentful and they cease to think or behave in a rational way. Fired by real hurts, their imaginations are quick to invent worse wrongs or to exaggerate existing ones without stopping to give anybody the benefit of a doubt or to ponder if they themselves might in any way be to blame.

The situation in the company was explosive when we arrived, and the early days of our management could best be described as a state of truce. After finding out what the principal gripes were, we went about setting things right. First, we tackled the parking-lot problem. We paved and illuminated the big lot and moved company Cadillacs out of sight. Once that was done, we turned our attention to the cold-water war and we traced the source of that difficulty in short order. We reported to the union committee that the lack of hot water was the fault of their own maintenance men, so it was a problem they could cope with themselves, any time they felt so inclined.

Before long, the firm was back in business, production was purring along at a record clip and the contract negotiations went off without a hitch. It seems incredible, doesn't it, that a thriving industrial plant can reach the edge of disaster through such simple misunderstandings? But this is a perfect example of the kind of misunderstandings that can fester and grow into major difficulties when corporate leaders are not responsive to the feelings and needs of their employees.

Most business managers know their technical specialties backward and forward and are pretty well informed on all aspects of their own positions, such as planning, reporting, and controlling. Where they fall down is in the field of developing people-potential.

A frightening number of high-level managers just don't have the slightest idea of how to get maximum efficiency and productivity from their work staffs. They either ignore them entirely (except, as I mentioned before, when they goof) or they tend to treat them like children. Neither approach is going to cut much ice with the boys in the back room. Like anybody else, workers like to be recognized as people, not just cogs in a production system. For starters, the foreman or executive who can remember men's names has a great advantage. Who doesn't appreciate that little salute to his individuality that a casual, "Hi there, Tom," or "How's it going, Jim?" can convey?

The men who remain remote to their personnel are, in the main, men who don't understand the effect this behavior is having on the other end. They don't behave remotely on purpose; they just have no idea how much resentment and disrespect this ivy-tower attitude can breed.

The ancient Greeks preached the dictum, "Know thyself," but we often ignore this advice today. Yet it remains one of the most important keys to successful management and as such, it is a prime goal of the laboratory sessions at ABS. We know that a man who knows himself—a man who is aware of his posture, his gestures and other behavioral patterns and the effect these have on other people—is best equipped for success in business and in personal relationships. For it is one's personal traits which have the greatest influence on how others react to one. And it stands to reason that the more positive the reaction, the better job can be obtained. You know yourself that if you like someone and respect that person, you'll go out of your way to please him.

A man I knew who owned a major publishing company in a New York skyscraper complained privately of his displeasure with his subordinates. "They're a bunch of rabbits," he said. "It's like pulling teeth to get any information or an idea out of them!" I made a mental note of his remark and set about convincing the publisher that a week at an ABS session might help him to find the answers to at least a few of his problems.

A Company Is Not a Building

Sometime later, the publisher attended a seven-day laboratory session in Ann Arbor. After a decent interval, I wrote to ask him what, if anything, he'd learned in the laboratory. The answer was characteristically straightforward: "I never knew what a son-of-a-bitch I was!" he roared over a long-distance line.

The fact was, he wasn't a son-of-a-bitch, but he sounded like one! He never talked to his staff people, he yelled at them—and as a result, he had cowed a complement of intelligent, responsive people into shivering pillars of silence. The shouting died down considerably at Ann Arbor, where the other members of the group made no bones about taming my publisher friend. For the first time in his life, he learned from the circle of strangers what his business associates—and even his family—had been too intimidated to tell him: He scared the hell out of everybody with his loud manner, and nobody could see through it, much less get through it to the sympathetic nature it masked. This honest reaction was only possible from people over whom he wielded no power.

People are our primary assets in business. Yet people are often far down on the list of management concerns, which are more apt in some cases to dwell on a flashy sign on the outside of the building, well-polished floors and plush office furniture. Why is this so? Easy. It's less trouble to polish a floor than it is to polish up one's human relations.

A small company in Illinois took to posting a guard in the entrance lobby shortly before five every afternoon, and he remained at this post until the last work shift finished at midnight. His job? To take care of a large vase of plastic birds-of-paradise in the lobby. Somebody (or bodies) had been systematically removing the enormous flowers from the premises. Seven had disappeared before the guard was posted, and management's only thought was to protect the flowers.

Management's first concern was to guard its property, without thought of the expense a nightly custodian entailed. It worked. The flower-pilfering stopped. But wouldn't it have made more sense to get at the bottom of the problem, to find out why people were stealing the flowers? It seems to me that the answer was obvious: Stealing the flowers was a worker's or workers' way of expressing resentment for something—maybe it was the vast amounts of money that had been spent on decorating the front offices, including the lobby. Everybody knew—and termed it a necessary economy—that corners had been cut in furnishing work and recreational areas of the plant—areas that were used constantly by workers, but would pass unnoticed by VIP visitors. Equal concern for both would have been the answer. Stealing the flowers could have been a way of getting back.

The brightest, shiniest-looking building or furniture is worthless, unless the human element matches it. It's especially noticeable in stores and restaurants—businesses where the element of "service" is as important as the goods which are offered for sale. Just think of some of the world-famous stores in New York, and everybody groans out loud. Some have the most comprehensive, exciting inventories of any city in the world, but you have to fight for the privilege of making a purchase. The sales personnel have reputations for "customers last" service. Fanciful window displays lure customers inside, and the merchandise is often worth fighting for, but how much better over-all profits would be if they could somehow get the message through to sales help that customers are people, too, and that not everybody has the time or the inclination to wait for two saleswomen to finish a lengthy conversation before being permitted to buy an article.

The importance of people to a business is especially apparent, too, in small businesses, where the personal touch means everything. A rural town I visit occasionally boasts a small, old-fashioned drugstore, where you can buy a soda or a cup of coffee while you wait for a prescription. It's a dinky little place, with an old-fashioned drugstore smell. A few years ago, the owner of the place —a delightful septuagenarian with no plans for retirement—was worried sick when he heard that a national drug company was planning to install a branch on the corner of his block.

He watched anxiously as the new drugstore was built —a vast emporium with huge glass windows, costly upholstered luncheon booths—the works. A year after its grand opening, the new drugstore, which had offered the townspeople a block of paperback books, a housewares counter and even a travel service, in addition to pharmaceutical staples, closed its doors and went out of business. The town preferred its own drugstore—and as a matter of fact, its own hardware store and its own bookshop to the homogenized operation of the national chain. All that glitters does not necessarily mean gold in the pocket.

A similar case involved a dry-cleaning company near one of my offices. A chain operation owned a shop on a busy corner of the city. It had been in business for a good many years, and the shop itself was nothing to brag about. It was clean, but otherwise dingy in appearance; yet it did as much business as any branch in the chain.

One day, a bright young vice-president of the parent company happened by. He was distressed by the appearance of the store, which to his eyes fell far short of the image the chain tried to project. Back he went to write a report to the president, recommending that the branch be brought up to date, architecturally. Since the young vice-president was the fair-haired boy of the outfit, his recommendation was taken, and before long, an architect and a decorator were hurrying on their way to the shabby cleaning shop.

Modernization is a weak word for the change they wrought in the ancient establishment. The worn wooden counter was replaced by a kidney-shaped structure padded in orange leather. Mirrored walls reflected the movements of pedestrians for blocks in either direction, and the glittering interior was bared to the world by the installation of wall-to-wall plate-glass windows. The young vice-president hurried around to inspect his baby.

His eye fell approvingly on the orange padding, the mirrored walls and the other improvements so clearly visible through the windows. It fell less approvingly on the manager of the establishment—an elderly, white-haired, pipe-smoking gentleman named Max, who had managed the shop since the 1930s. The vice-president took in the manager's baggy pants, his old-fashioned suspenders drawn over a checked woolen shirt, the neat bow tie that completed his ensemble. Max decidedly did not match the new look of his shop.

The vice-president, who was not a very sentimental

A Company Is Not a Building

soul, wrote another recommendation, and as a result, Max, to his great surprise, was pushed gently but firmly into retirement. A shiny young manager was found to take his place, and the vice-president was happy at last. His contentment was short-lived.

Six months later, the company's sales charts showed the renovated branch to be slipping drastically. Profits were off by almost 25 per cent. Hurriedly, the sales staff dug into the records for the names of customers, and conducted a telephone inquiry to unearth the cause of the slippage.

The answer they got was simple and unanimous. The customers missed Max. He knew their names and a good deal about their lives and would chat with them during business lulls about the weather or current events, or their families. Some customers had long since moved from the neighborhood, but had continued to bring their business back to Max for the sake of his friendship as much as the expert cleaning services the shop had to offer. When Max went, they started trying more convenient cleaning shops.

What had struck the young vice-president as the fly in the ointment—the person who didn't fit in—was actually the key to the whole operation. Max was a caring human being whom no amount of interior decoration or architectural improvement could supplant.

It's natural and understandable to take pride in one's physical surroundings—to be pleased with thick carpets on the floor and one's name on the door and all that sort of thing. But we should save our special care for the people with whom and for whom we work, because they are the number one asset of any enterprise.

VIII. Taking Personal Inventory

How many times a day do you look at yourself in a mirror? At least a dozen times daily, most of us check our reflected images. Is the tie straight? Is the hair neat? Is the makeup in place? We are extremely conscious of how we look and of the effect a pleasant or unpleasant appearance has on others. Are we as conscious of the other invisible, but just as important aspects of our persons?

Too often, we are inclined to accept the book for the cover, in spite of the old adage warning against such a practice. It can be a dangerous mistake, taking people at their face value. I knew a millionaire who wore a shabby suit everywhere—even to formal dinner parties, and a well-dressed con man with apparently excellent credentials (including an expensive wardrobe and all the other outward signs of well-being).

To know ourselves and to judge others fairly, we must consider the whole man—not just the façade that greets the eye. As we have pointed out before, the laboratory trains its participants to recognize the true nature of others in the group—to spot the true worth of others and themselves. The behavioral science laboratory helps its trainees to develop a keener awareness of their own character and a knowledge of how certain traits strike others. This knowledge enables them to modify their behavioral patterns and to become more effective persons, once they have left the lab.

But as with any consciousness-raising process, there is a built-in danger of a letdown after the fact. It's hard to maintain the self-searching impulse on your own, without the support of the group or the pressure of the group dynamic to keep it going. The intensity of the laboratory experience simply cannot be carried over into one's everyday life. It's too exhausting, it would burn out the strongest, most energetic person within weeks. But the self-searching impulse—the inclination toward awareness and understanding—must be maintained if the laboratory experience is to have any lasting value for the participant.

To facilitate the formation of a continuing pattern of self-assessment, we've devised a lapel pin we call a PI (for Personal Inventory) Coin. The name has a double significance, for the coin also resembles a pie which has been cut into five slices. Each slice represents an aspect of the whole person—an aspect which should be inspected periodically and adjusted, if necessary, to provide maximum performance. The five aspects of a person represented by the five segments are: appearance, personality, integrity, intelligence, and status.

As we've indicated before, appearance is not the whole story—not by a long shot. But it is a vital part of the whole, and as such, cannot be ignored. It might help if we clarify what we mean by "appearance," so that the term will not be confused with beauty or "looks." If beauty is only skin deep, it is also what you're born with—or without. Appearance is what you make of yourself, what you do with whatever degree of beauty you possess.

Obviously, you don't have to have the face of a movie idol or a model's figure to achieve a good, acceptable appearance. It's more a matter of doing the best with what you have, of good grooming, cleanliness, and the ability to choose attractive and appropriate attire for any occasion. As an added advantage in getting ahead in the world, appearance cannot be downgraded or underestimated.

Appearance is a frequent topic of discussion during laboratory sessions at ABS. A man in his thirties, attending a lab in Ann Arbor, constantly vented his anger at the rest of the group. He seemed to be mad at the world. He was an extremely intelligent fellow, but his disappointment at not getting ahead in his work had turned to a blazing core of bitterness. He worked on the office staff in the advertising department of a high-circulation women's magazine.

What he really wanted to do most was to sell space for the magazine, a job that entails going out of the office and making contacts with all kinds of prospective advertisers. He had all the attributes that would ordinarily insure success in this kind of job. He was a fascinating conversationalist, he showed flashes of real wit, and he had no trouble striking up easy acquaintances with strangers. A natural, you'd imagine, for the front office and beyond. Only one thing wrong—he looked like ten miles of bad road.

Even during the session, where everyone is encouraged to wear comfortable, informal clothing, this man's idea of informal was everybody else's idea of a real mess. His hair was combed once a day, badly, in the morning; and his fingernails were unmanicured, to put it politely. It was glaringly obvious to the laboratory group that the only thing holding this man back was his untidy appearance, and they told him so.

It took a while for the message to sink in. The habits of a lifetime cannot be overcome overnight. But the man made a special effort during the remainder of the week to improve his appearance. He was still no Don Juan, but his nails were clean and trimmed, his hair got combed three times a day instead of just once, and his tie was miraculously free from greasy stains and spots. He'd gone as far as he could go to make himself more attractive physically, and he could count on his personality to do the rest. It had an impact back in his office, as might be expected. A few weeks after leaving the laboratory, our man reported back triumphantly that he was at last being given a chance to prove his skill at selling space for the magazine.

Having taken his appearance as far as it would go, this man could depend on his personality to win his battle for a chance to sell, which brings us to the second piece of PI—personality. But first, I'd like to stress that the purpose of this coin is to help every individual to achieve a PI balance that will work for him. It stands to reason that not everybody can score 100 points on each of the five counts. Nobody—or at least relatively few of us—are incredibly good-looking, packed with personality and integrity, highly intelligent, and resting comfortably on the tops of our professions. All those attributes just don't turn up in equal doses in the average person. Everybody has some good points and some bad—in the case of the would-be space salesman, his personality made up for a less-than-perfect appearance, but he didn't think he was attractive and just let his appearance go. Somebody else might be able to coast along on a less-than-engaging personality if he or she had the intelligence to cope skillfully with special technical problems. In the case of a bank teller, obviously the combination of intelligence and integrity would be of topmost importance. In any case, the average person's PI goal should be to achieve a balance that will help him or her to achieve his or her personal goals; and also, to make it easier to ascertain that he or she is doing the best possible in each of his five pieces of PI.

Personality is another word that's hard to pin down.

Taking Personal Inventory 135

One dictionary definition, "Magnetic personal quality," seems closest to the mark of what we mean on the PI coin. We talk of people getting by on their personalities, but that isn't strictly true. What the phrase probably indicates is that personality plays a very important part in that person's success, that it overshadows other aspects of the person's makeup.

There's a luncheon counter near my office—a fairly large place, with several jutting counter areas. It's packed solid at lunchtime on weekdays, and one particular counter is packed even when the rest of the place has emptied out. The reason? The waitress who takes care of that counter—a not-so-young lady named Claire, whose personality draws customers to her section like moths to a flame or flies to honey. As waitresses go, Claire is not about to win any prizes for speed, efficiency, or beauty. But she is always cheerful, and greets every customer she knows with a smile and a word of sincere greeting. Her unruffled good humor is a boon to tired office workers. She cheers people up. And her marvelous personality pays off in more customers and more tips than any other waitress in the place.

That's how personality can work for you. A bad personality sometimes works just as dramatically against a person. I used to visit one of my offices with a vague sense of reluctance—a milder form of the malaise that sets in as you set out for the dentist. It puzzled me, because there were no particular business problems connected with that office, and I couldn't figure out why it bothered me so very much to go there.

One day as I stopped to shed a wet raincoat in the

reception area, it dawned on me. The receptionist was a real pill. She was a good-looking girl, she dressed well, and she seemed to be bright enough. But she had a really tough, negative personality. She never smiled, and she addressed visitors as though she were doing them a favor by talking to them. I figured that if she had that effect on me—her boss—she was probably treating our customers and business associates to the same.

An insurance salesman almost drove everybody crazy during the week he spent participating in a laboratory session. In and out of his group, he complained constantly. If it hadn't been so annoying, it would have been funny. He complained about the room he'd been assigned, he complained about the roommate who shared it, he complained to the roommate about other members of the group, he complained about the food. He was a born, chronic complainer. Under pressure from the group, he began to see himself as others saw him. He was intelligent enough to understand that he should try to correct this habit, of which he'd previously been blissfully unaware. His first attempts were rather comical: He'd complain about the weather, for instance, but he'd smile while he did it! When he got home, he made a point of trying to check himself, every time he felt like complaining. It took a lot of self-control, but it was worth it. Among other things, he learned to save his complaints for important situations. But the biggest change of all took place in the man's personality. Once he abandoned the role of professional griper, he emerged as a pleasant, companionable man. Others began to take pleasure in his company, whereas before, they'd avoided him like the plague.

A pleasing personality won't insure a brilliant future, but it's something everyone should strive for—if for no other reason than because it makes life so much pleasanter for the person who has it and others around him. Without a passably pleasant personality—unless you're a nuclear physicist or similarly specialized—you're working against a disadvantage. And chances are if two nuclear physicists, equally brilliant, were bucking for the same research post and one had the better personality, he's the man who would get the job.

Although the PI coin is divided into five equal parts, the slice labeled Personality should perhaps be larger than the others, for it truly holds the key to the other four. It is possible for a person to get a fairly good idea about those other four qualities without the aid of a lab. Not totally, of course—the lab helps you develop every aspect of your personal inventory. But there are ways for you to determine and improve your appearance, intelligence, and status outside a lab, and even integrity can be developed without reference to the sort of situation a lab offers.

But personality? How can a person know himself unaided? How can he even know himself through social relationships, where dishonesty is the common lubricant? The lab experience homes in on personality at once, and pries at it relentlessly until it opens up like a flower. And that's when remarkable things begin to happen. The changes filter into the other areas of the human character until they too yield their full potential. People who were careless about their appearance, or always seemed to dress inappropriately, begin to look at themselves in new ways and strive to present a more appealing aspect both to themselves and others. Intelligence, though innate and basically unchangeable, at least begins to focus on problems that have lain fallow or unexamined all these years. New attitudes toward status may develop—you may aim higher if that is what you truly wish, or you may become less anxious about it, or more accepting of your position in social or organizational situations. Integrity too is affected because you are able not only to look at yourself more honestly, but to stand behind your decisions instead of copping out as perhaps you've been doing and disliking yourself intensely for it.

Third, we come to the piece of PI that can't be subdivided—integrity. This is the one area of one's personal makeup where no compromise is allowed. If you haven't learned the value of integrity by the time you're an adult, you're in bad shape to begin with. And none of the pieces of PI will do you any good at all unless you are capable of applying this integrity to the process of self-evaluation.

The one form of lying that we accept relatively calmly is self-deception. Perhaps because it's self-directed and therefore, self-destructive, we don't generally label it an offense against society. But if we lie to ourselves, we are holding ourselves back and reducing our chances of fulfilling our potential—and that hurts society. The laboratory experience teaches us to face the truth, however surprising or unpleasant it may be, and to utilize this truth for self-improvement.

Taking Personal Inventory 139

The woman dean of a southern college discovered at one ABS session that she'd been lying to herself for years about the reasons she had never gotten married. She had to take care of her aging mother, or at least that's what she told herself—and anybody else who was rash enough to inquire. Of course the truth was, she was just using her mother as an excuse to avoid marriage. Her mother, although elderly, was perfectly capable of caring for herself—and would, as a matter of fact, have preferred to do just that. Her daughter's pose of "unselfishness" was actually a wall of selfishness which gradually imprisoned the older woman as well as the daughter.

It must be understood that people who punish others for honesty will force those around them to be dishonest. Also, cruel honesty is stupidity because it negates caring—one of the most essential ingredients in a constructive society.

Sometimes, we limit our chances of success by lying to ourselves about our obvious limitations. The world is full of embittered people who rail at imagined obstacles and enemies, who never can own up to the fact that they have done or are doing the best of which they are capable—that the reason they haven't gotten any further is that they can't do better than their best. Self-knowledge enables us to set reasonable goals for ourselves and attain more personal satisfaction by meeting those goals. So the big question behind the "integrity" piece of PI is: Am I really being as truthful as I can be with myself, as well as with others?"

Shakespeare put it this way, "This above all: to thine

own self be true, And it must follow as the night the day, Thou canst not then be false to any man."

Intelligence, you may think, is a set commodity—one which is bounded by the limits of a person's Intelligence Quotient. But if you equate intelligence with the capacity and power of understanding, you can easily see how we can improve this commodity in ourselves as we go along. The most intelligent person in the world, in terms of I.Q. ratings, can behave stupidly in a given situation, unless he exercises the intellect indicated by his I.Q. to further his own understanding of himself and the people around him.

What good is a brain if you don't use it? Most of us don't use our brains to the utmost, even on a good day. The laboratory training session shows us how to stretch our minds to greater understanding in all directions. We learn things about ourselves we hadn't guessed at before. We learn to listen carefully to other people and to learn more about ourselves from them.

Two Detroit businessmen who attended two different sessions reported back practically identical reactions later on. An investment specialist said, "I am now more willing to listen to people I might have categorized as 'insignificant.' I have learned that everybody, no matter what he looks like or how you might be tempted to label him, has something to teach." A young banking executive put it this way: "The biggest hangup in my career was bucking the system—fighting people who were just part of the woodwork. Now, I'm more sensitive to how they feel. I'm wiser and smarter about my approach to these people, even though my basic aims are the same as before."

What is self-awareness if not knowledge? The lesson that emerges time and time again from the laboratory experience is how often a lack of awareness about our own behavior prevents us from understanding others as well as we might. One of the most common expressions heard throughout the laboratory experience is, "I never realized that!"

The publisher who barked at his employees and the policeman who laughed at long-haired youths both learned something—and as a result, became more intelligent—during their laboratory sessions. The publisher who didn't know what it was like to be afraid of anybody, was made to realize that he frightened people and that his staffers were handicapped by fear of his gruff manner in their dealings with him. The cop realized that the hippie was proud of his beads and his hairdo and became recalcitrant when these personal status symbols were mocked.

By putting "intelligence" on the PI coin, we don't mean a person has to take an I.Q. test every few weeks. We only mean that he should try to remember the lessons learned in the laboratory and to add to them—and his powers of understanding, or intelligence—by continuing to seek to improve his awareness and understanding of himself and others.

Lastly, we come to the subject of status—a perfectly good word that has fallen into bad repute. We've been conditioned to sneer at "status seekers" and "status symbols." Okay. Admittedly, both phrases have a phony ring. Generally speaking, they refer to people who are seeking "status" or its outward trappings for purposes of social advancement. Yet there is nothing wrong with real status.

Webster calls status the state or condition of a person. We like to take that one step further and call it a man's achievement. Is there anything wrong with being proud of your level of achievement? It's a prime indication of how you're doing, the sum total of the effects of the other four PI ingredients, and if you don't know how you're doing, how can you do any better?

An old friend of mine is one of those unfortunate, middle-aged executives who lost their jobs through corporate cutbacks in early 1971. His qualifications were outstanding, yet a year after being fired, he was still job-hunting. Why? Because during his career, he neglected to keep track of his status level.

The man I'm talking about is well above average in many ways. A superior intelligence has been apparent since his school days. He is a person of unquestionable integrity. His personality is affable and engaging and his appearance is impeccable and attractive.

What did he do wrong? He stayed in a dead-end job too long, at too low a salary for a man of his combined talents. Call it a lack of ambition, or maybe just plain laziness. It doesn't even matter which it was, the effect was the same. He liked his job, it allowed him a good deal of leisure time, which he enjoyed idly; and he was not a greedy man—he managed to get by on his salary. Why should he push for more?

It may be a sign of creeping materialism, but it's also a fact of life that today's corporate managers measure prospective employees by these mercenary values as well as by their proven abilities. If a man isn't aggressive enough or proud enough to demand what he's worth, there are others who will—and they're the ones who get the prizes.

And so it behooves us not to neglect status, much less sneer at it, as we check our Personal Inventories. We must make sure we're doing as well as we know we can, and we must pursue our goals boldly and energetically to keep in step with our potential.

There's no magic about the PI coin. It's just a handy reminder—like a five-finger exercise—to help the wearer take inventory of himself from time to time.

Even if you don't have a PI lapel pin, you'd do well to remember the five pieces of PI and what they stand for. Check yourself from time to time. Make sure you know and utilize your good points. Recognize and try to improve your weak points. By taking personal inventory and acting on your findings, you'll be a happier and more effective person, and most important, more in control of your destiny.

IX. You've Got to Start at the Top

The dignity of a staid large bank was shattered one morning when a junior executive walked into the office of his boss and gave him a bear hug. In the confusion that followed, the junior executive attempted to explain that he was just trying to express his gratitude for a memorandum his boss had written, commending the younger man for his work on an important trust agreement. But as he explained to a friend over martinis that evening, the effect would have been the same if he had handed his boss a bomb.

You've Got to Start at the Top 145

To onlookers at the bank, whose reactions ranged from simple amusement to severe shock, it appeared that the junior executive had suddenly gone berserk. The truth was, he had gone too far in applying a lesson he'd learned during a laboratory session at ABS. In terms of the ability to express his emotions freely, he was light-years ahead of his boss, thanks to the laboratory lesson. But his boss just wasn't ready for it!

Unfortunately, the episode of the unwanted bear hug serves to illustrate the most important point concerning the laboratory adventure. There is absolutely nothing to be gained by exposing middle-management men to the laboratory experience and expecting them to be able to work miracles back on the ranch—be it a bank, an industry or a campus. It would be the same as training children, then sending them home to practice the lessons of behavioral science on their parents! In the case of the happening at the bank, it took the impulsive junior executive several weeks to earn back the confidence of the senior vice-president he'd embraced—a difficulty that might not have arisen had the senior vice-president shared the experience of a laboratory training session.

And so, the actuality turned out to be a disappointment to the younger banker. An action which he had intended to produce a very positive effect instead provoked two negative results. The elder vice-president, even when mollified, modified his approval of the younger banker and henceforth regarded him with a large grain of skepticism—as somebody to "keep an eye on." And the junior man, chastened by the fuss, modified his own behavior, taking a giant step backward from where he had found himself at the end of an extremely exciting and successful laboratory experience.

It happens all the time. There's an inevitable clash —a kind of conflict of intent—between the laboratory trainees and the people to whom they return who have not had the benefit of the laboratory experience. It happens in schools and it happens in homes—but nowhere is it more visible than it is in the world of business.

Daniel Webster made the remark, "There is always room at the top," referring to his chosen profession, the law. And we can bend this famous quotation to our purposes by adding the words, "for improvement." There is always room at the top for improvement, and the plain truth is, the top is where any significant plan for improvement of any kind at any level must begin. This is because of another hard fact of life which applies to business or to any administrative situation: If the boss doesn't like an idea, you can be pretty sure it isn't going to work!

Perhaps more than any other kind of innovation in personnel training, behavioral science methods must start at the top. In the home, this would mean a parent; in a police department, the chief; on campus, the college president and administrative staff as well as acknowledged student leaders; and in business or any other institution, people from the very top administrative levels. To introduce the laboratory training experience at any lower rung of the organizational ladder is, to say the least, quixotic.

An executive trainee or other junior employee who participates in a training session may actually reap greater personal rewards than an older person with less flexible views. He or she will emerge from the laboratory experience full of new ideas, with a new and exciting awareness of his or her own behavior, a greater understanding of the behavior of others, and a much greater ability to really listen to what other people are saying. These are the general learning goals for all who attend an ABS training laboratory. It stands to reason that to set an ABS "graduate" back in the middle of a management chart without any support or understanding from his superiors in terms of what he has learned virtually deprives him of these newly acquired tools for self-improvement. He can't use the lessons he has learned because none of his co-workers is similarly enlightened.

In Gian-Carlo Menotti's famous Christmas opera, *Amahl and the Night Visitors*, the young beggar boy, Amahl, has a terrible time convincing his mother that there are three kings standing at the door of their humble abode, requesting shelter for the night. The young business executive, enlightened but isolated by his laboratory adventure, faces a similarly frustrating position.

He is confronted with the difficult and sometimes downright impossible task of convincing "older and wiser" heads of his organization of the benefits that could be accrued from application of the lessons he has learned in the laboratory. He is just like Amahl, pleading to be believed that there are three kings at the door. But to add to his difficulties, his "three kings" are not readily demonstrable, as Amahl's were, consisting as they do of ideas and visions of a more harmonious and productive business operation.

I tend to talk in terms of corporate life because the world of business is, frankly, my turf. But it should be stressed that the word "management" extends far beyond the walls of the biggest business corporation. From our point of view at ABS, it is applicable to any group situation in any area of human endeavor.

There are managers (teachers and principals) in schools; managers (mothers and fathers) in families; managers (chiefs, captains, and lieutenants) in police departments; managers (drivers) on buses; managers (deans and student leaders) on college campuses; managers (administrators) in hospitals; and a myriad of other managers, including those in hotels, restaurants, and stores who actually use the word as a title to identify their positions of authority. The laboratory training experience can be applied to advantage in any of these situations, at any of these management levels. It can be used to improve understanding and strengthen relationships between husbands and wives, or to open avenues of communications between parents and their children. In fact, some of the most dramatic results of our work at ABS have occurred in areas outside the corporate community.

During a particularly intense session at Ann Arbor, a middle-aged broker launched into a raging tirade—an angry discourse on the faults of the younger generation. They were arrogant and unheeding, he declared angrily, and they isolated themselves from the rest of society with their confounded airs of superiority. They had no respect for their elders, and they thought they had the answers to all the world's problems long before they ever had to confront the world's realities.

You've Got to Start at the Top

The rest of the group listened patiently as the man stormed on. It was obvious that his speech had been prompted by somewhat flip observations of a younger member of the group—a graduate student from a nearby university. So the young man apologized and tried to calm the older man down.

As the broker's wrath subsided, a calmer discussion of his views took place, and during the course of this discussion, a vital fact came out: The man's own seventeen-year-old daughter hardly ever spoke to her father. Instead, she retired to her room directly after dinner every evening, and emerged in the morning for breakfast. There were no friendly family chats in front of the fireplace—the family didn't even watch television together! At meals, the daughter confined her conversation to polite requests to pass the butter. She seldom, if ever, made any contributions to the general dinner table talk.

With the group's support, the broker was faced with a new reality about himself and was finally led to see what he hadn't been able to see all by himself—that his daughter's attitude stemmed from the fact that he never listened to what she had to say when she did speak to him. What he had considered conversations with his daughter had actually been lectures—sometimes even sermons—directed at the girl. She was never invited to reply or questioned as to her views, and her answers, when she bothered to give them, were largely ignored or overridden by her father. Quite reasonably, she decided that talking to him was a waste of her time, and she finally gave up trying.

Armed with this new knowledge about himself, the broker went home from the laboratory session with a markedly different attitude toward his daughter. The evening he returned, the two of them sat together until three o'clock in the morning, deep in real conversation. This time, however, the broker did most of the listening, and his daughter did most of the talking. The result was inevitable: a new and much more satisfactory relationship, a new level of loving between father and daughter, and a new understanding and happier family structure all around.

It worked because the father was the manager. He was in a position to effect a change in his relations to his daughter. But you can imagine how futile the laboratory experience would have been if it had been applied to the daughter, instead.

No matter how much support and understanding she might have received from her group, it would have been lost when she returned to her home life. If her father never listened to her in the first place, it's a lead pipe cinch he was not going to succumb to her new ideas, which in his old, non-thinking way he probably would have labeled "newfangled nonsense" or ascribed to the general, lamentable follies of today's youth!

The laboratory adventure is a rich and exciting one for those who partake of it. In a short week, they learn more about themselves than they may have learned in a lifetime. They also learn to listen. But the laboratory is, alas, powerless to teach this same lesson to those who aren't present. It's practically impossible for a single trainee to transmit all the learning experience to others.

In the words of the old vaudeville routine, "You hadda be there!"

To be able to listen, to be aware of one's own behavior, to be able to freely express one's feelings—whether they are feelings of anger or of affection—these are the most important, the most beneficial lessons of the behavioral science laboratory experience. And it is all but impossible to attempt to filter them upward. They can only filter down through a business organization, an institutional hierarchy, or a family.

We mentioned the plight of the young banker who tried to please his boss by hugging him. A similar disillusionment lay in store for a civic-minded socialite from Chicago who tried to share the lessons she had learned at an ABS session with her superiors at a voluntary organization back home.

The leading lady in this drama was the local chairman of a national volunteer organization in her community. For several months, on two afternoons each week, she had been driving her gleaming station wagon into the heart of the black ghetto area of her city. There, she spent hours at a neighborhood center, helping underprivileged youngsters to improve their reading skills. She had been trained to teach remedial reading, and there was no doubt from this point of view about her ability to do a good job at this kind of work.

But for some time, this civic-minded lady, while conscious of "doing her duty," was plagued by the notion that things weren't going as well as they might. The children were not responding as quickly or as well as she had hoped they might (and knew they could). To her dismay, the whole project was beginning to look a little hopeless.

While attending a laboratory session at Ann Arbor, the volunteer was given a whole new view of herself and the effect her appearance had on other people. To her astonishment, she discovered that she came across as a "snob." That she really wasn't didn't matter. Even the group discovered eventually that the woman unconsciously projected this image as a cover-up for extreme shyness. But the woman herself realized that the small children with whom she dealt had no way of understanding this. She had been coasting along, thinking that as long as it was fairly easy for her to relate to them (they were, after all, just children), it followed that they should have no difficulty in relating to her.

After the laboratory session ended, the woman returned to Chicago bursting with new ideas and eager to try them out. She was anxious to get back to work and to try some new approaches—some of which had been suggested to her by her recent laboratory friends. Up until that time, she had unthinkingly worn rather expensive clothes—even some jewelry—when she visited the ghetto center.

Now, she put on an old sweater and skirt and took a bus to the ghetto neighborhood. She alighted a block from the center and walked the rest of the way. She also took a few minutes before the remedial reading class got under way to chat with the children—something she had been too shy to try before. Within just a few weeks, the results of these simple changes were happily apparent. The children's learning progress had improved dramatically, and the volunteer herself was getting much deeper satisfaction from her job as a result.

Not content with her own little triumph, the woman sought to pass along the lessons which she had learned. Painstakingly, she wrote a detailed report of her experiences both at the behavioral science laboratory and the neighborhood center, and sent it to the regional director of her organization. She included suggestions on how other volunteers could improve (or at least tone down) their "lady bountiful" images as she had done. Sadly, the director decided not to act on any of the woman's recommendations. She wrote a polite letter, saying that she felt that in a voluntary organization, matters of dress and the like should be left to the discretion of the individual volunteer and not made a matter of policy. She concluded that instructions of this nature lay beyond her domain.

Discouraged by the official reaction to her report, the local chairman resigned her post in protest, continuing her work with the neighborhood center on a private basis. Once more, the message failed to get through because it was sent in the wrong direction. What a different story might have been told if the regional director had been the one to attend the lab session and see the light!

An international investment organization prepared a report for its board of directors, a report based on the laboratory experiences of several of its principal officers. The organization was preparing to incorporate ABS training on a broader plane as part of an advanced personnel program; and the report stressed the importance of starting at the top, pointing out that "over-all company benefits will be substantially enhanced if the first groups to attend ABS laboratories include very high-level personnel."

Time and time again, our experience has shown us that to dip below the top administrative levels in the beginning phase of laboratory training is totally useless. Middle-management men are like army veterans returning from the war to civilian life, where their courageous battlefield actions are belittled and even scorned. Middle-management men go back into the old culture of their organization and what they do is to ram right back into that same old stone wall. Unless they are understanding, those in authority above them can—and often do—destroy any program they propose. "Too idealistic," they'll say, or, "We haven't got time for that kind of nonsense around here."

On the other hand, there is no limit to the size of the miracles you can work by starting at the top. We sincerely feel that by working with the ten top people in any organization in the world, we can demonstrate a dramatic improvement in the thinking structure of that organization. It isn't just that the top men are in a position to impose their will on their underlings, although that is certainly the case. It all goes back to that old business about being able to lead a horse to water. You can't make anyone understand the tenets of behavioral science if he doesn't want to. But a good manager who has experienced the laboratory adventure and believes in the good that can come of it can also sell the idea and pass it down the line until it permeates the entire organization.

A large insurance company provides a good corporate example of the benefits that can be reaped from proper laboratory training, properly applied. I managed to convert the president to the cause of behavioral science, and to introduce ABS methods, he sent his executive vice-president for sales and marketing to a week-long session in northern Michigan. This man was the very model of a modern business major general—a man who seeks out and uses every tool he can command to make his men more effective managers and marketers. So he gladly accepted the challenge.

The experiment was a huge success. "I wish that all of the key men in our sales department could attend one of your training laboratories," he wrote in a letter. "I know that once men can work together with complete honesty and empathy, the solution of our business problems would come easily."

With both the moral and financial suppport of his company president to smooth the way, the company started sending men to ABS sessions. First, he sent seven divisional vice-presidents—the men who run the company's sales operations in various sections of the country. The results were extremely beneficial, and they were twofold: A tremendous improvement in both the morale and honesty levels of the seven men; and a noticeable increase in insurance sales.

District managers, the next echelon of sales department executives, were the second group to go. The results of their attendance again served to reinforce the already enthusiastic attitude toward laboratory training and the good it can do within a business corporation—particularly a corporation that sells a service, rather than a commodity.

The vice-president testified to a markedly improved honesty level in his own department. "Those who have had this training are no longer telling us what they think we want to hear, but what they really believe," he says. "This is what good management wants—not 'yes-men,' but honest men." It really is the most sensible way of running a business.

The testimonials from this company alone could fill their own book and they all have the same, glowing tone. A divisional vice-president made this observation: "There seems to be a dramatic change in the attitude of the 'bosses' as well as the 'bossed' after they have been through a lab. Our 'bosses' seem to get more out of their men now that they express greater interest in them as people, rather than as just numbers on the organizational chart."

The quality of subsequent sales meetings reflects the total value of the laboratory trainees' experience. "There is an atmosphere of greater trust, friendship and cooperation," says the vice-president. "All of us find it easier to accept criticism without taking it personally. Also, some of our quietest people have become freewheeling personalities because they are no longer fearful of reprisals for speaking their minds. Above all else, I am convinced that nothing, but nothing supplants intellectual honesty in the successful operation of a business." It's a valuable message that can work wonders in any organization—it doesn't have to be an insurance company—but it has to work its way down through the organization. It's kind of like building an ice cream sundae. You wouldn't think of putting the chocolate sauce on the bottom of the dish and covering it with ice cream. You put the ice cream in first, cover it with the sauce, and let the goodness run down over the whole thing!

Under most existing management systems, the low man on the totem pole has hardly any choice of making his voice heard, however good an idea he may have. And in most cases, he refrains from honest criticism because he knows that such action, virtuous though it may be, is often unappreciated by those on high.

If middle men, or even those on the bottom rungs of the organizational ladder, are given to understand that honesty is a good policy—that honesty will be rewarded or at least appreciated by the boss—they will give that boss honesty. But the boss has to start the ball rolling.

X. Love Thy Neighbor—and Thyself

Everybody needs to love and to be loved. It's not a luxury. Even in the Computer Age, love remains a staple of our lives—a vital force that still "makes the world go 'round."

For a time, it seemed that we were forgetting about love, in our haste to acquire a second car and a summer house. But the rising popularity of sensitivity training and all kinds of encounter groups clearly indicates that love is making a comeback—perhaps in reaction to the necessary computerization of practically everything and everybody. We live in dehumanizing times. The individual has been reduced to a fat pack of cards, each card bearing a longer number than the card before. Our identities have been flattened out and printed on bits of paper—social security cards, credit cards, banking signature cards. Try renting a car without a credit card, and you'll discover how completely these paper identities have replaced traditional values, including hard cash.

For years, the man in the street has concerned himself solely with the attainment of material success. He has scrambled to get that second car and a house on a lake. And he has been so busy running and reaching for the brass ring of affluence that he has had no time (and has made no time) to think about love. Finally, when the car and the vacation pad have been attained and a spiritual emptiness persists, he has turned his thoughts back to love—he is thinking about it in a big way and pursuing it just as relentlessly as he ever pursued success, by plunging into laboratory sessions, T groups and other, similar self-discovery safaris.

The need for love is very great, and so it requires great means of fulfillment. Now that we are sufficiently affluent to pay attention to our psychological needs, the laboratory training session presents an ideal method of helping people to meet these needs. It's like a concentrated dose of love. It satisfies a hunger for something the person cannot find elsewhere—even in his family, or in his church. It provides an opportunity for people to have close and real relationships with other human beings under circumstances in which feelings and emotions can be freely and spontaneously expressed and accepted.

In the laboratory group, within the circle of anonymous equality, the necessity of censoring one's feelings or stifling an emotion is removed. Extremes of disappointment and joy can be experienced fully and shared with the others in the circle. One is encouraged to experiment with new ways of behaving, to take risks without fearing the consequences. Given this total freedom of expression, the individual approaches the point where total knowledge and total acceptance meet, and it is there that further spiritual and emotional growth can begin.

Throughout the ages, poets ranging from Catullus to Rod McKuen have written millions of words on the subject of love. It has probably inspired more literature than any other human emotion. Yet most of this literature—and in particular, the poetry—generally tends to treat love simply as a philosophically esoteric topic. The laboratory experience brings love to life as a "gut" happening—something for the whole man, instead of an idealistic tidbit to tickle his fancy, or his vanity. The laboratory experiences teaches man that love—far from being the self-sacrificing ritual described and glorified by poets—is a two-way street.

Perhaps a more realistic and accurate definition of love can be found in this formula:

$$Love = Caring + Fulfillment$$

In other words, love requires an honest caring for someone plus the personal satisfaction which derives from that caring. A giving and an accepting. Caring, of course, is the truest and most valid expression of love. The real lover, the person who is capable of experiencing love best, feels real concern for the loved one—concern for the loved one's pain as well as for his joy. By caring, the lover reaches out to the loved one and gives. He expresses his caring through the giving of warm and spontaneous affection to another human being. A person who honestly cares is able to attend to the needs and wishes of another and to see these needs and wishes clearly. Caring is the giving part of love.

But love is also fulfillment—and by this, I mean satisfaction for oneself. The lover must be accepted for himself with warm, spontaneous feelings. He must be recognized as a person who can relate to others out of respect—respect for them and respect for himself. He must be cared for.

All those poets and songwriters speak of "giving one's heart" to the loved one, and the myth persists that in loving, we are giving away or losing a part of ourselves, as if depleting a stockpile of good feelings. That is simply a poetic notion, and it has nothing to do with a true love process. In truth, the true lover benefits enormously from the loving experience. He is satisfied by the knowledge that he is acting in a wholly natural, human way to create a meaningful interaction with another human being. It is only natural that this knowledge fills him with confidence and self-esteem. Now, he can love himself even more, because he sees things clearly and he understands himself to be really lovable.

The concept of unselfish love is just as unrealistic as the idea of "giving away" one's good feelings. The greatest fallacy is that true love is, or should ever be absolutely altruistic—that man should aspire to a state of selfless caring, without expecting or even wanting anything in return. But it's little wonder that we cling to this notion, because we've heard it all our lives. It's the theme of many a tired, moralistic motto; it is, for example, implicit in the biblical advice to "turn the other cheek." It demands the impossible of a human being, because it demands total regard for the interest of another (or others) and at the same time, a complete disregard for one's own interests. This is even harder to do than patting one's head while rubbing one's stomach. It goes against man's very nature.

Man is well documented as a creature who naturally desires and requires fulfillment. One of his most basic psychological needs is to be emotionally completed, to be fulfilled, to be given something by somebody else which he cannot supply for himself. Should we be surprised at the consequence of this strange concept—that faced with these contradictory terms, man has become emotionally confused?

On the one hand, we recognize man's desire for and drive toward fulfillment. But on the other, we preach that he can attain this fulfillment only by being selfless—by totally disregarding his very desire for fulfillment. The poor guy can't win.

Man's emotional plight is similar to that of a racing greyhound, who streaks feverishly around a track in pursuit of a stuffed, mechanized rabbit he can never catch. Man is made to feel guilty for having natural drives and desires over which he has absolutely no control, for they are an inherent part of his nature.

Children reared according to the teachings of this pious, doctrinal double-talk grow up with poor self-images. They are told that they should be a certain something—a self-denying giver of love—and they discover than no matter how hard they try, they cannot be that something. The desire for fulfillment persists, lurking in a corner of their emotions. Painful frustrations set in as they try repeatedly to attain the unattainable goal of selflessness. Finally, they begin to blame themselves, to look upon themselves as failures; and they become emotional invalids, unable to love or to be loved.

Groucho Marx once made a very funny joke about refusing to join a certain country club because, as he put it, he didn't care to belong to any club that would stoop to accept him as a member. And that's roughly what happens to a person who has been raised in the school of "selfless love": he can't make the grade, so he can't love himself—and as a result, he cannot love anybody, because he cannot create an effective interaction of caring with another person.

Every single one of us has a unified, well-defined set of standards and propositions which make up our self-identification or self-image. As this self-image crystallizes, it forms an invisible, cell-like room around a person. This invisible room can be small, indeed, for it represents the self-imposed limitations beyond which a person cannot even attempt to reach. A man becomes locked into the restrictions of his own perception of what he can realistically expect of himself, and as a result, his potential is reduced to the limits of what he believes he can do.

Starting with this essentially negative self-image, a person is hampered even further by the fact that every decision and action must penetrate this motivational block. Take a man who is burdened with doubts, convinced that he is generally incompetent and as a result, deserves little. A man who is so weighted down will deny himself the luxury of trying. Inevitably, he will pass judgment upon himself with more severity than anybody else would use in judging him, so his self-image is a good deal lower than the image he manages to project to others.

This perpetual process of self-condemnation is an extremely unhealthy practice of our society, but it is also a very common, widespread practice. We render ourselves emotionally impotent, incapable of accepting honest love and concern because our self-image denies to us the fact that we are lovable.

If a man does not trust himself, he cannot trust other people. However strong his instincts, his self-image remains his most immediate reference point. He is hampered by the fact that he can only act like the kind of person he thinks he is. So he cannot have love and respect for others if he cannot manage to love and respect himself. And others, in turn, will not be able to love and respect him because, by acting in accordance with his poor self-image, he announces to the world that he is unworthy of love and respect.

Loving may be a natural emotion, but it doesn't just grow, like Topsy, without any care. The fundamental ability to love depends entirely on two factors: self-esteem and self-respect. It all goes back to the same idea: Before an individual can love another, he must be able to

Love Thy Neighbor—and Thyself 165

love himself. To achieve perfect love, we must forget all those notions about unselfishness. To love oneself is not, as our past teachings would insist, a sign of selfishness, conceit or egotism. It is a basic necessity of total love.

If an individual falls into the habit of devaluing himself, how can he place true value on others? If he cannot bring himself to accept his own strengths and weaknesses, how can he possibly manage to accept the strengths and weaknesses of others?

We should strive to love ourselves. To be capable of loving oneself implies a regard for oneself as a human being and the confidence that comes with the possession of a sense of self-value and self-importance. Those who can love themselves don't have to prove their worth. They are not compelled to impress or manipulate other people. They don't have to worry about "ego," they suffer no illusions about the measure of their own significance, nor do they use other people to achieve their own ends or attain shallow status goals.

A person who loves himself respects his own integrity, so he has no need to violate the integrity of anybody else. Asserting his own rights and dignity enables him to respect the rights and dignity of his fellow man. It's what Shakespeare meant by "to thine own self be true," which you notice he enjoined to be placed "above all."

It all seems quite obvious when you think about it, but most of us are taught to believe that self-love is wrong. This misguided teaching probably stems from the misplaced notion that self-love is related to selfishness, when in reality, nothing could be further from the truth.

There is nothing in the teachings of any of the world's major religions which even suggests such an idea.

Many of these religions teach us that we should love our neighbor as ourselves. You notice—not more than ourselves or instead of ourselves—*as* ourselves. The message is clear: Man should have respect for himself and he should love himself. He has no moral obligation to degrade himself, to make any excuses for living or for taking up space in a world he is destined to direct toward good.

For reasons that defy explanation, our society has cultivated an attitude of guilt as a staple of everyday life. The policeman, the minister, the parent—all of these influential figures seem to appear to the young in roles that are permeated with guilt and punishment. As a result, we are nurtured in a lopsided fashion and we grow up with a very one-sided view of love.

Our natural egos demand that we accept man as the pinnacle of creation. Yet if man really is the pinnacle of creation, he must have respect for himself. Whenever he fails to have such respect, he is being untruthful, he is failing to see himself in a clear light. He cannot possibly be integral, honest or real if he does not act respectfully in interrelating with other people. He must strive to share himself as he is—a respectable, important, unique individual. If he does this freely and with honesty, he should be received respectfully and freely—and from this he can derive fulfillment—a personal interplay which is satisfying to the lover as well as it is to the loved.

If a relationship falls short of this and fails to provide such fulfillment, it is not a truly human experience at all,

Love Thy Neighbor—and Thyself

but rather, a misguided and uncreative distortion of truth. Nobody should be expected to enter freely into a relationship which reduces him to something he is not —which treats him untruthfully.

Balance is the master key to achieving a true love relationship, and when the balance fails, there is a serious danger of too much self-love. This can hamper the ability to love as badly as a lack of self-love. A person in conflict over his own needs for attention and acceptance will have little energy or impulse left over to take care of another love relationship. He winds up working extra hard to protect himself from anxiety, and in this way he prevents himself from seeing others as they really are. A man in this condition is looking primarily for fulfillment, without the caring. What he fails to realize is that the more he cares, the more he will find fulfillment. He misses the all-important point that a person who is capable of loving is free to care. Such a person is able to see other people as lovable individuals with all the strengths and weaknesses we all share.

An uneasy balance means that love becomes less easy. When a lover's need for fulfillment outweighs his ability to care, his love becomes selfish as a consequence. The would-be lover then becomes insecure and introverted, and this reversal manages to frustrate the natural process of fulfillment.

As the songwriter wrote "Love Is a Simple Thing." It really is. The greater the caring, the greater the fulfillment. It is only when the fulfillment becomes more important and overbalances the caring that love ceases to be a fulfilling process.

The fulfillment that a person finds in love has a therapeutic effect on his whole being. Perhaps the most basic fulfillment of all is the achievement of perfect communication with other human beings. The key to perfect communication is having maximum awareness of one's own feelings and the feelings and perceptions of other human beings. It stems from a person's awareness of himself—of his own self-actualization, self-determination, and commitment. Self-acceptance, self-esteem, and self-confidence also facilitate the communicative process.

Man's basic integrity prevents him from becoming absolutely altruistic. He realizes in spite of himself that he cannot behave in a completely altruistic manner and and at the same time fulfill himself by loving naturally as a dignified human being. A man is less than a man if he fails to have a genuine interest in and concern for himself.

Man finds fulfillment only when his interrelationships with others earn him their respect and concern. He receives fulfillment only when his caring for other human beings branches out of concern and respect for himself. Loving is an active process where the lover reaches personal fulfillment and the deepest satisfaction through his concern for the self-fulfillment and satisfaction of another human being. The fulfillment and satisfaction of another person becomes as significant to the lover as his own fulfillment and satisfaction. Thus, we have the golden rule: Love thy neighbor as thyself. Not more, or less —*as*.

Laboratory training has no more important lesson to teach than how to care for oneself and others. It is a lesson that is learned again and again in the course of the laboratory adventure—and often as not, it is learned by people who thought they had all the answers.

But embarking on this adventure calls for a measure of courage. In a lab you will be facing five or ten years of concentrated problems, and it is, in the hippie phrase, a "heavy trip." Thus you must be unafraid to join a group, unafraid to face a roomful of strangers, unafraid to submit yourself to their criticism, and above all, unafraid to change. Does this mean you have to be a hero? Of course not; courage comes in quantities considerably smaller than hero-sized. But who is to say what heroism is or how it is earned? If it is defined as bravery in the teeth of challenge, or determination to conquer the unknown, who of us is not qualified to be a hero?

The barriers between people can be as high as a mountain, as treacherous as the open sea, as full of unknowns as outer space. Overcoming them may not be as sensational as crossing the Pacific in a rowboat or voyaging to the craters of the moon, but the satisfaction is no less. To break through a communications wall, to earn respect from a person whose respect is worth earning, to accept a critical remark about yourself without hurling up your usual defenses, to throw yourself into the growth process instead of shrinking as you've always done—this should be heroism enough for anyone.

A business executive named Jerry summed it up after participating in a training group. When he introduced himself to the group at the start of the session, he had made a point of declaring his independence. He needed no friends, he had proclaimed proudly. But as the session wore on, he realized how false that statement was—how deeply lonely he really was, and how great a need he had to be accepted. He saw that he needed to be part of what was happening to other people. He described his discoveries like this:

"Well, the first thing I think of is that it is possible to have other people reach out if you in turn will reach out to them. I mean it is possible for this to happen, and it is a feeling of becoming closer to people—especially to individuals. I don't know why I struggle to say this. The only thing I can relate is this feeling that happened to me regarding Beth's problem and then the response from Roz—they immediately seemed to take me back into the group, or back into the human race. I guess you would say, back into other people's feelings. They are concerned, and people can be concerned about you, regardless of who you are."

That's what the laboratory experience is all about.

Appendix

INSTRUCTIONS

STEP I—DATA COLLECTION

After the problem has been presented each ten-man team breaks into two five-man subteams. The subteams should be established on the basis of choice. Every member of the subteam then writes his 5 ideas or solutions to the problem on the sheet provided in this pamphlet. Each man's ideas are then collected and consolidated into one list of 25 ideas. Invariably there will be duplication among the 25 ideas.

The five-man subteam, after discussion, reduces the 25 ideas to only 5. This is the consensus of the five-man subteam.

Suggested time 1 to 1½ hours.

STEP II—EVALUATION

The two five-man subteams now meet together and are once again a ten-man team. Each five-man subteam will have one list of 5 ideas. These are combined on the worksheet provided and each idea or solution is reviewed. The ten-man team analyzes the ideas and solutions and reduces the list of 10 to the 5 most important ideas.

Suggested time 1 hour.

© No part of Shared Participation may be reprinted, copied or used in any way without the express permission, in writing, of American Behavioral Science Training Laboratories.

STEP III—CONSENSUS

The individual voices of the team are now one voice; a further consensus has been reached. Each ten-man team then selects one member to represent them in presenting their 5 ideas to management. Here again, it should be emphasized the identity of contributing members remains undisclosed. The team has one voice, its representative.

STEP IV—COMMITMENT

Each ten-man team representative is now ready to approach management with his team's 5 most important ideas or solutions. This presentation is made in the presence of all team members, but only the representative is to confer with the management panel.

The team representatives and management will discuss the solutions submitted. They will reach agreement as to action to be taken. If new information is presented by management it may be necessary for the team representative to confer with his team for further instructions. It is possible new information will alter a team's recommendations. After misunderstandings have been resolved a consensus between management and the team representative has been reached. Then a commitment is made by team member to team member, team member to management, management to team members, and management to management. Each is committed to act upon the recommendations made. A timetable will be established for the implementation of each idea. Responsibility for follow-through will be assigned by management and team members.

STEP V—FOLLOW-THROUGH

Team members and management now have an obligation and a commitment. A review meeting will be held in three to four weeks to examine results. Additional review meetings may be scheduled as necessary.

WORKING EXAMPLE

As a working example, a production problem of *quality* is presented for SP teams.

Step 1. Data Collecting—In the general meeting of all ten-man teams, it is explained that the quality problem has become so serious that production schedules are not being met, deliveries to customers are x per cent below customer requirement, scrap is x per cent above normal, rework is x per cent above normal and at standard cost, and the product is showing x per cent loss instead of x per cent profit. A solution must be found to correct this situation, or the company will have to give up this product, which would result in discharge of x number of employees.

This problem, having first been explained to the ten-man teams, is referred to each ten-man team to come up with ideas or solutions by first dividing into five-man subteams. Each member of the five-man subteam writes down his five most important ideas or solutions on how to solve the problem.

Appendix

Each five-man subteam now has a total of twenty-five ideas or solutions—each member's five ideas consolidated.

First Subteam's 25 Ideas or Solutions:

1. Wrong steel
2. Too hard steel
3. Too soft steel
4. Wrong analysis of steel
5. Not heat-treated steel
6. Wrong gauge of steel
7. Undersize steel
8. Incorrect cutting tools
9. Not hardened cutting tools
10. Not properly sharpened cutting tools
11. Incorrect design of cutting tools
12. Poor supplier of cutting tools
13. No carbide cutting tools
14. Machine worn—will not hold tolerance
15. Machine will not operate at proper feed
16. Machine will not operate at proper speed
17. Machines have too much slop
18. Inspection gauges are worn
19. No inspection of steel for gauge and size
20. No inspection of steel analysis and hardness
21. No inspection of resharpened tools
22. Poor design for method of manufacture
23. Chambers need a radius for undercut
24. Operators not properly instructed for precision work
25. Operators did not know amount of scrap

Second Subteam's 25 Ideas or Solutions:

1. Poor quality of steel
2. Steel limits too great to make the product
3. Steel should be heat-treated

4. Steel analysis should be changed
5. Cutting tools not designed properly for the product
6. Carbide cutting tools needed
7. Should not use reworked cutting tools because of critical limits
8. Dull cutting tools being put on the job, both new and reshaped
9. Machines will not hold the critical tolerance
10. Machines need rebuilding
11. Machines do not have proper drives for feed and speed
12. Machines are not the proper machines to make the product
13. Not enough inspection gauges to check all critical limits
14. Inspection gauges are not properly made to correctly measure the critical limits
15. Steel should be gauged before released to production
16. Steel analysis is not checked to be sure it is the correct analysis
17. Not enough trained inspectors
18. Too much inspection is required by the operator for this critical product
19. Every tool should be inspected by engineering
20. Engineering should redesign the machines and tools used to make the product
21. Product could be made if engineering would recalculate the critical limits
22. Bumping up operators due to seniority causes green operators to be on the most critical operations
23. Training program should be set up to instruct all operators on the critical dimensions
24. Operators just don't give a damn
25. Scrap should be charged back to the operators so they would be responsible for their work

Appendix

From the examples of the two subteams, it can be seen that many of the questions raised by both subteams overlap, although worded differently, which is a natural expectation.

Still within the framework of Data Collecting and Evaluation, each five-man subteam selects the five most important ideas or solutions which they feel would correct the *quality* problem. Much, MUCH, M U C H discussion and problem solving follows with new understanding by every member.

First Subteam

1. Heat-treated steel
2. Correct gauges
3. Inspect cutting tools and only put on job proper tools
4. Rebuild the machines
5. Engineering add dimensional relief for manufacturing in main critical areas

Second Subteam

1. Change analysis of steel, including adding heat-treat
2. Redesign the cutting tools, including the use of carbides
3. Rebuild the machines so they will hold proper tolerance
4. Rework gauges to proper tolerance
5. Train operators for the product and impress upon them that they are making a *quality* product

Step 2. The two five-man subteams now meet as a ten-man team to reduce the foregoing ten ideas to the most important five—which is further evaluation.

1. Change analysis and heat-treat steel
2. Redesign and make new carbide cutting tools
3. Rebuild machines to hold tolerance
4. Make new easy operating gauges
5. Train operators

Step 3. Based on these five most important ideas or solutions, the ten-man teams, having reached a consensus, then select one member to represent each ten-man team to speak for them to management—each representative having been a member of the team and properly briefed as to the reasoning by the entire membership of the team.

Step 4. The entire ten-man team attends the meeting between their team representative and management, but only the team's representative speaks to management, making the presentation and giving the reasoning for the team's decision.

The management team for this example is composed of approximately the General Manager, Plant Manager, Foreman of the Manufacturing Department, Purchasing Agent, Chief Engineer, Chief Inspector and Sales Manager, totaling about seven men representing management in their respective areas.

After much discussion in depth between management and team representative, a consensus is finally reached on each idea or solution presented, and a time schedule is set for implementation of each idea or solution, with a specific employee selected to follow through.

Time	Individual
1. Two weeks	Chief Engineer and Purchasing Agent
2. Two weeks	Chief Engineer and Purchasing Agent
3. Three weeks	Plant Manager
4. Two weeks	Chief Inspector and Plant Manager
5. Two weeks	Department Foreman

In this manner, a commitment is made by both team and management through the team representative, with the implementation and responsibility for implementation.

Step 5. Follow-through is established by setting up a review meeting in three or four weeks, followed by a second and third review if necessary to make sure the time schedule is being met as set by those responsible.